W9-BVG-100

Advance Praise for
In Search of Authentic Faith

"Steve Rabey is one of our most reliable culture crunchers, distilling swelling movements and trendy tidbits into a sensible grid for his readers. *In Search of Authentic Faith* is Rabey at his best. Drawing from myriad sources, he seeks the heart of true Christian faith at the millennium, the sort that 'cuts through the complexities of culturized Christianity and allows what is primary and essential to surface.' Rabey understands the material he discusses, not only intellectually, but also actively. His personal walk reflects the truths surfaced in this book."

—JOE MAXWELL, senior editor of *re:generation quarterly*
and editor of Reformed University Press

"If ministry to the Next Generation has seemed like a ragtag assortment of weird experiments—a random spray of dots on a map—Steve Rabey's *In Search of Authentic Faith* masterfully unpacks the weirdness and connects the dots: geographically, historically, philosophically, and culturally. Get ready for the light bulb to go on."

—SALLY MORGENTHALER, author of *Worship Evangelism:
Inviting Unbelievers into the Presence of God*

"With *In Search of Authentic Faith*, Steve Rabey has painstakingly employed his intrepid research skills, putting together a volume that not only includes insights from just about every major player in this wild subculture called the modern church, but also presents their thoughts, opinions, and stories in a way that makes sense—and makes for great reading."

—DAVE URBANSKI, editor of *Youthworker Journal*

"Finally, a book that moves beyond the bewilderment and hand-wringing that characterizes so much of what evangelical boomer pundits have written about the seemingly inscrutable ways of Generations X, Y, and Next. Steve Rabey's *In Search of Authentic Faith* shows how the emerging generations have already begun to reshape North American Christianity. While this book is certainly valuable reading for those who desire to minister to younger people, it is equally important for anyone who wishes to understand where the church is headed in the twenty-first century."

—LARRY ESKRIDGE, associate director of the Institute for the Study of American Evangelicals, Wheaton College

in search of
authentic faith

How Emerging Generations
Are Transforming the Church

steve rabey

WATERBROOK
PRESS

IN SEARCH OF AUTHENTIC FAITH
PUBLISHED BY WATERBROOK PRESS
2375 Telstar Drive, Suite 160
Colorado Springs, Colorado 80920
A division of Random House, Inc.

ISBN 1-57856-319-4

Published in association with the literary agency of Alive Communications, Inc., 7680 Goddard Street, Suite 200, Colorado Springs, CO 80920

Library of Congress Cataloging-in-Publication Data
Rabey, Steve.
    In search of authentic faith : how emerging generations are transforming the church/
  by Steve Rabey.—1st ed.
    p.   cm.
  ISBN 1-57856-319-4
    1. Church work with young adults.   2. Generation X—Religious life.   I. Title.

BV4446+   00-043870

Printed in the United States of America
2001—First Edition

10 9 8 7 6 5 4 3 2 1

contents

the church of the future begins now

Perhaps you are one of the many people wondering what shape and direction the church will take during the twenty-first century. Or perhaps you're eager to see how emerging generations of Christian leaders have been remaking the church. Or maybe you simply want to know what has become of all the spiritually hungry young people who seem to have made a mass exodus from both traditional and contemporary congregations.

During the 1990s, hundreds of articles and books examined the many ways in which the Western world's philosophical moorings and generational makeup were undergoing profound changes. In this book we will examine some of the many new churches and underground ministries that have emerged in response to these cultural changes.

Of course, the people and groups profiled on the following pages could change direction more than once between the time these words are being written and the time you read them. Change has been a constant throughout Christian history, and the pace of change has kicked into overdrive during the last decade or two.

The chapters that follow attempt to provide a guided tour of the changing face of Protestant Christianity in America at the dawn of the church's third millennium. This tour begins with a look at two recent efforts that couldn't be more different from each other, but each in its own way demonstrates something about the staggering diversity that will come to characterize tomorrow's ecclesiastical landscape.

A Gen X Megachurch

Twenty-one-year-old Trevor Bron wasn't setting out to make church history in 1993 when he launched a simple evening service called Tuesday Nite Live, which was geared toward college students and met in the small chapel of Applewood Baptist Church, a Southern Baptist congregation in the Denver suburb of Wheat Ridge. Bron's emphasis on "good music and relevant teaching" and his single-minded focus on reinventing the church for his own generation struck a chord with the area's Christian young people—many of whom had fallen through the cracks at other churches—along with some of their unchurched friends.

Within two years, as an official history puts it, this tiny group "grew from a handful to a crowd." Today, that crowd varies in size from fifteen hundred to nearly two thousand—and most are young people. It's largely because of such numbers that many young leaders have come to view Bron's experiment as the model for the future of the American church.

In the early years, this new, youth-oriented ministry was about as far away from the cutting edge as one could be. A 1996 edition of *Xcitement*, the group's newsletter, included offbeat tips on "How to Handle Stress":

"Jam 39 marshmallows up your nose and try to sneeze them out," or "Find out what a frog in a blender really looks like."

But at the same time, Bron and his Tuesday Nite Live ministry were developing an increasingly passionate sense of calling to an emerging group of people many observers referred to as Generation X.

"What is TNL [Tuesday Nite Live]?" asked the ministry's newsletter. "It's a Generation X thing.

"What is Generation X? It's a generation of young adults who have been stereotyped as slackers, but who really are the best hope for the future. So TNL is a 'church' for Generation X. It's laid back, contemporary, and relevant."

In his "From Pastor X" column, Bron stressed the importance of creating a close-knit Christian community. "TNL [is] more than just a gathering of unknown people," he wrote. "It's a place for a family to gather."

Like many in his generation, Bron had grown up as a latchkey kid accustomed to spending much of his time alone, and he harbors ambivalent feelings about families. He was raised by his mother and had little contact with his father, an alcoholic who, when Bron was three years old, left the family and died seven years later. "What little I did see of him was very threatening and intimidating, for the most part," Bron recalled.

His personal pain and memories of family dysfunction resonate deeply with other young people who, regardless of their upbringing, place a premium on friends, companionship, and community. "The driving force behind Xers' lives is relationships," Bron observed. Not surprisingly, more than five hundred of TNL's members participate in church-sponsored small groups.

By 1997, Tuesday Nite Live had been re-christened as The Next Level Church. The group had outgrown Applewood Baptist's small chapel and had even maxed out the church's much larger sanctuary. Now they were meeting in—and almost filling—the auditorium at Crossroads Church of Denver, where upwards of eighteen hundred members of the so-called Generations X and Y were singing their hearts out during half-hour periods of rock-oriented worship music. But that's not all. They also were furiously scribbling notes during Bron's sermons, many of which were verse-by-verse expositions of selected biblical passages.

By 1999, TNL was enjoying a growing reputation as America's largest standalone Gen X church. Christian leaders from around the country were flocking to Denver to study its methods and learn from its twenty-something staff, much as earlier generations of leaders had flocked to Chuck Smith's Jesus-movement Calvary Chapel or Bill Hybels's seeker-sensitive Willow Creek Community Church to experience the latest "next new thing."

TNL also boasted a topnotch Web site (www.tnl.org) and a growing line of products, including worship music CDs and organizational manuals. Its staff members were invited to speak at national ministry conferences. Many pastors hoped that TNL had developed a winning formula for reaching a generation that, in many churches, was being overlooked.

Rich Hurst, a baby boomer and Colorado-based church consultant and author, serves as an adviser to TNL. He pointed out that the congregation provides a vital service to other congregations that are desperate to find a way to reach younger people. "Most churches have programs that meet the needs of boomers and middle-aged people," said Hurst, "but they have little that meets the needs of the average young adult, making this population the most unchurched and unreached portion of American society."

Today, at a growing number of places like TNL, emerging young believers are remaking the church for the new millennium.

"Our goal is to be as accessible as we possibly can and to adapt to our ever-changing culture," said Bron, TNL's senior teaching pastor. "The message of the church should never change. But culture changes, and what worked in the fifteenth century isn't going to work in the twenty-first century."

Like hundreds of other TNL regulars, twenty-nine-year-old Heather Kobielush doesn't know much about ecclesiology or church history, but she loves attending church with other members of her generational cohort. "I appreciate the fact that I can worship with people my age who are serious about their faith," she said. But Kobielush also appreciates TNL's outward-looking emphasis on community outreach and service. "They have really helped develop a desire and passion to serve others even further," she added.

An Itinerant Iconoclast

If TNL is the successful public face of the emerging Christian generation, Andrew Jones represents its idiosyncratic apostolic underground. Like TNL, Jones is making history, but relatively few people have heard of him. Throngs don't flock to see what he's doing, which would be impossible, since he has no fixed location. Most of the time he is on the road in a Winnebago with his wife and four children, crisscrossing the country on his itinerant outreach to dozens of elusive Gen X ministries in college towns and urban centers around the country.

One day finds him in the Northeast, where he is meeting up with a group of young people who minister at raves, the high-decibel, drug-drenched, all-night parties that have become meeting places for many of today's youthful hedonists and neo-pagans. Like Jones, the Christian ravers travel in an RV, but theirs is equipped with a high-tech sound system and turntables. With dreadlocked hair and a communal lifestyle, these modern-day musical missionaries would receive a cold shoulder at most churches. But they aren't trying to impress church people. Rather, they seek to reach those who are far beyond the reach of traditional churches.

Another day finds Jones meeting with a small group of believers in the Midwest who host regular poetry gatherings in a downtown coffee shop. People of all faiths—and no faith—bring and read their own verse, which explores a wide range of subjects, from the silly to the sublime.

On yet another day, Jones is meeting with a southern California couple who run a vintage clothing store during business hours and operate a small artists' colony during their free time. The artists aren't required to sign a statement of faith—the organizers believe creativity is a God-given gift and that exercising this gift will bring a person closer to the Creator.

Occasionally, Jones lands in one place for a spell, as he did for part of 1998 in San Antonio, Texas, and 1999, when he and his family were based in the San Francisco Bay area. While in the Bay area, he worked with a group called the Prodigal Project, a ministry to countercultural kids that *Charisma* magazine called "a hippie monastery." But Jones also became involved in numerous other ventures, some of which were chronicled in a report entitled "Godspace 4: The New Edge," written by Golden Gate Baptist Theological Seminary's Brad Sargent (www.ggbts.edu/continuum/unplugged.html).

But most of the time, Jones is on the go. People keep track of him through the Internet, e-mailing him at a "CyberRev" address. Even though Jones uses the latest communications technology, he draws his inspiration from the early church. His methods look like a latter-day version of Ireland's seafaring Celtic monks, some of whom sailed the high seas without oars, sails, or tiller, relying instead on the hand of God to guide them. As Saint Brendan the Navigator put it, "Is not God the pilot and sailor of our boat? Leave it to him. He guides our journey as he wills."

Jones explained: "Basically, our ministry is making friends, telling stories, and throwing parties. We are a circle of friends that is becoming a global neighborhood of spiritual leaders who are trying to find a new way of doing church.

"We are developing a new way of gathering [ecclesiology], going [apostolic ministry], and empowering [training]. We are attempting to create a support system for a network of organic, relational communities of believers who download the kingdom of God to where it is needed most."

In Austin, Texas, Jones helped organize a rave event at a local church. The event received positive reviews from both the local daily newspaper and the city's alternative weekly, the *Austin Chronicle*, which crowed, "Held inside a 75-foot-tall labyrinth designed along the lines of Dante's *Divine Comedy*, you'll experience a multidimensional, multisensory service like no other church you've ever been to."

Part networker, part matchmaker, and part apostle Paul to a diverse and geographically scattered group of potential Timothys, Jones often works with people who have e-mailed him. At other times, he goes to a town and starts snooping around.

"Every city has a creative, alternative area," he explained. "I just ask around, and somebody will know." Once there, Jones starts looking for signs of spiritual life. On occasion, a local pastor will know about someone involved in a creative outreach, but most of the time the folks Jones knows are too avant-garde to pass muster at the local churches.

"These ministries are not attractive," he observed. "None of them have one thousand people attending worship services. Most of them don't even have worship services. And they certainly don't have big-name leaders that people call about writing books or speaking at their conferences. Many of these people don't even get a salary from their ministry."

In fact, some of the ministries with which Jones interacts aren't even aware of other groups in their own area. Over one three-week period, Jones received e-mails from three separate Atlanta-area believers who had a passion for reaching the residents of the city's Little Five Points area. Jones introduced these believers to one another and brainstormed with them about things they could do together.

Making connections between these cutting-edge ministries is one of the things Jones feels called to do. "A lot of these new ministries have more in common with what the early church in the New Testament looks like than they do a large, well-financed church or organization," he said. "But God has given us all freedom to minister in different ways."

Jones believes these hidden groups stand at the forefront of a movement that will transform the way the church carries out its ministries in the twenty-first century.

"I have become more convinced that our focus should be on the work of the kingdom and that church planting just happens as a result of that," he asserted. "These emerging ministries are part of a new reformation of ecclesiology and methodology. They are finding a new language for expressing the gospel."

In Search of the Future Church

For nearly a decade, observers of the North American church scene have been investigating and debating the generational and philosophical changes confronting churches. In 1986, Dieter Zander founded New Song Church in Covina, California. At that time nobody was using the term "Generation X," but Zander could tell that a new group was emerging. As he wrote in a 1999 issue of *re:generation quarterly* magazine, "We were encountering the leading edge of a generation who processed information differently, were cynical about the integrity of established organizations, and were deeply committed to their friends—characteristics that have now been well documented by sociologists."

In 1992 pollster George Barna published *The Invisible Generation: Baby Busters,* the first book-length study on the subject by a Christian thinker. By 1995 both Zander and Barna had written new books on the subject. In 1996 they joined nearly two hundred other key emerging young leaders who descended on Colorado Springs for a conference on ministering to Generation X. The event was one of the first such national gatherings, and the participants pointed to problems in the contemporary church scene, even if they weren't sure what forms and changes should follow.

"For many of the nearly forty million young people between the ages of eighteen and thirty-four," said Ken Baugh, "preachers are like used-car salesmen or politicians." Baugh is director of Frontline, a ministry to baby busters at McLean Bible Church in McLean, Virginia, which is one of the nation's biggest and most influential congregations geared toward younger believers.

Barna and others helped alert Christian leaders to the emergence of post-modernism (see chapter 3) and argued that pastors and preachers would need to tap into the power of stories to communicate with new generations of listeners.

"This is our first postmodern, post-Christian generation," said Barna. "They've been immersed in the philosophy of existentialism and the view that there's no objective reality. They're very nonlinear, very comfortable with contradictions, and inclined to view all religions as equally valid. So the nice thing about telling stories is that no one can say your story isn't true."

Kevin Ford, an evangelism consultant (and nephew of Billy Graham), agreed. "Find the stories behind the [biblical] passages," he told the group. "Don't destroy a good narrative by breaking it up with points. Just tell a story. And don't explain it. That's condescending."

Some of the young leaders at the 1996 conference went home to launch dozens of new congregations and ministries. Others had already done so. Although some of these initiatives have died, others have continued to evolve and mature, taking on new and unexpected forms.

"We're in the middle of a transition period, and nobody knows what the church of the future is going to look like, or even if there is such a thing," observed Ron Johnson, the founding pastor of Pathways Church in Denver.

Now is a good time to survey some of these efforts and see what this emerging group of leaders has learned thus far.

A Reader's Guide to This Book

Dozens of books have explored the theories of ministry to Generation X, but none has explored the ecclesiastical terrain and provided a portrait of some of the hundreds of emerging churches and ministries that may be our best indication of the shape that tomorrow's church will take. Such a survey is the primary goal of this book.

In the next two chapters, we will look at what some of the leading thinkers and observers have been saying about two major aspects of the future church: first, the emerging generations of young people who feel that most traditional and contemporary churches fail to touch them; and second, the ways that postmodernism has impacted theology and culture.

Then we will look at the ways in which a few core values of the emerging generations are influencing their views on life and ministry. Over the course of six chapters, this section will examine how values such as authenticity, community, religious experience, and pop-culture literacy have shaped the ecclesiology of the new leaders. We also will note how the views and experiences of these emerging leaders have played into the design of the new churches they are creating.

In the final section, we will examine some of the questions and tensions that have surfaced as the emerging leaders have struggled over the decision either to attempt to breathe new life into older ecclesiastical institutions and structures or to set out on their own. We will also observe how various denominations, parachurch organizations, and other evangelical institutions have addressed the shifts taking place in the rapidly changing religious landscape.

Finally, we will address the issue of leadership, for even though many of these emerging leaders aren't waiting around for people to show them the way, many of them would like nothing better than for mature believers to come alongside them and help them find their way.

You will meet dozens of visionaries and read about new churches and organizations that have been created to meet the needs of the future. Admittedly, this guide will be sketchy at best, and much of it will be out of date by the time these words are printed on the page. But this being the Internet age, we will provide you with much of the information you will need to continue your journey of discovery from various Web sites set up by these churches and organizations. At the end of the book, I will list some of the best available resources.

My prayer is that you will find this guide to be intriguing and inspiring and that this book will contribute to the ongoing renewal of the mystical entity known as the body of Christ.

part 1

new generations
in a new world

generating generations

A Brief History from Moses to Madison Avenue to Megachurch USA

A decade ago, hardly anybody used the term "Generation X," even though it was coined in the 1960s. By the mid-1990s, terms like "Gen X" and "Gen Y" were omnipresent in the worlds of retailing and religion. Today, however, some observers believe that these terms are already dreadfully passé.

Inquiring minds want to know: Where did all these generational labels come from? Who created them? And what, if anything, do they really signify?

In looking at the generations, the first thing one realizes is that those who treat terms like "Generation X" or "Millennial Generation" as if they denote clearly definable groups are in for a big surprise. There is strong disagreement about what separates one generation from another or how large each group is.

For example, the author of a 1999 *Wall Street Journal* article described Gen X as the forty million people born between 1965 and the late 1970s. Other sources, including Vann Wesson's irreverent book *Generation X: Field Guide and Lexicon,* describe the group as the seventy-nine million people born between 1961 and 1981. Other writers have added their own definitions of this group's age, size, and buying power.

There is even greater disagreement over the evaluations various analysts make of the up-and-coming generations. Perhaps Pat Robertson isn't more skeptical about Generation X than are other leaders of his generation, but the Christian broadcasting mogul certainly expressed his utter disdain in the most uncompromising terms. Writing in his 1993 jeremiad *The Turning Tide: The Fall of Liberalism and the Rise of Common Sense,* he unleashed his invective on the younger generation:

> We are seeing what is called the generation of "baby
> busters" growing up with no hope, no goals, no moral con-
> victions, no sexual identity, no feelings of patriotism, no
> identification with society, and no peace or even a capacity
> for happiness. It is one of the most pathetic groups of
> people that has ever come up in the history of the world.
> These are the people who are going to become our future
> leaders. On the average, they have no religious faith to
> speak of, and they have no realistic concept of God.[1]

But Todd Hahn, a young Presbyterian pastor who founded Warehouse 242 congregation in Charlotte, North Carolina, after ministering for years within an existing church, feels much more hopeful about the group Robertson dismissed. "In spite of its painful past and uncertain future, we believe that Generation X holds almost unlimited hope for the future of the church and the world," Hahn and David Verhaagen wrote in their 1996 manifesto *Reckless Hope.*

Generations in the Bible

Even more confusing is the way people casually toss around the term "generation." We'll spare you the detailed academic debates over etymology here, but understanding humanity's ever-shifting attitudes toward defining the generations is an important prerequisite to developing a meaningful approach for ministering to younger people.

There are half a dozen Hebrew, Greek, and Aramaic terms that, over the centuries, have been translated as "generation" in English versions of the Bible. Few of these terms bear any similarity to what contemporary Americans mean by the word.

The book of Genesis, for example, makes nearly a dozen references to "generations," but typically these refer to genealogical histories of a particular family or clan. These references reflect the high value given to the bonds of family and kin in ancient Jewish culture.

In Genesis 17, when God announced his covenant with Abraham, it was clear that the covenant extended to all those who would follow in Abraham's lineage: "I will establish my covenant as an everlasting covenant between me and you and your descendants after you for the generations to come, to be your God and the God of your descendants after you" (verse 7).

In later Old Testament books, the term "generation" can refer to a rather generic sense of olden times, as we find in the prophet Isaiah's proclamation of salvation for Zion: "Awake, awake! Clothe yourself with strength, O arm of the LORD; awake, as in days gone by, as in generations of old" (51:9).

The word also can be used to criticize the sad spiritual state of the Jewish nation. Just before the death of Moses, God gave the patriarch a foreshadowing of Israel's coming disobedience, a theme that Moses echoed in

17

his farewell song to his people: "They have acted corruptly toward him; to their shame they are no longer his children, but a warped and crooked generation" (Deuteronomy 32:5).

Christ made similar use of the term when he referred to his own contemporaries as a "brood"—or "generation"—of vipers (Matthew 3:7, 12:34).

Later, the apostle Peter described all who are followers of Christ as a chosen generation, or people: "But you are a chosen people, a royal priesthood, a holy nation, a people belonging to God, that you may declare the praises of him who called you out of darkness into his wonderful light" (1 Peter 2:9).

Still, most scholars agree that when biblical writers were describing the time elapsed between the beginning of one particular generation and the next, they typically understood this to be a period of roughly forty years, which was about the same amount of time Israel spent in its wilderness wanderings.

Subcultures for Sale

In the twenty-first century, the length of years between generations has been reduced from a biblical four decades to a more manageable two decades. And in some cases, any reference to biblical ideas of lineage has been dismissed altogether. Gary McIntosh's 1995 book, *Three Generations: Riding the Waves of Change in Your Church*, defines a generation as "a group of people who are connected by their place in time with common boundaries and a common character."

Not surprisingly, much of the impetus for defining the generations in narrower ways has nothing to do with Moses or mating habits, but it has everything to do with consumer goods and pop culture. Product manufacturers and marketers find it financially beneficial to define a profusion of often superficial subgroupings, which enable them to sell more of everything—from suds to duds—to more buyers. The ways in which baby boomers are differentiated from Gen Xers, who are differentiated from members of Generation Y, aren't under the direction of theologians or sociologists but rather marketers, who are trying to sell more goods by proclaiming the existence of generationally distinct submarkets.

In the 1990s, marketing to Generation X made many boomers rich, and by the mid-1990s, many Gen Xers were cashing in on the phenomenon of generational marketing. Steven Grasse, the then-thirty-one-year-old subject of a 1997 profile distributed by the New York Times News Service, admitted that his Philadelphia-based advertising company, Gyro Worldwide, was in the business of helping companies exploit the ever-shortening "life cycle of hipness."

"Most people get onto things when it is way too late," wrote Grasse, whose company had done work for MTV, Coca-Cola, and R. J. Reynolds Tobacco Company's Red Kamel brand. "The life cycle goes from obscure to cutting edge to mainstream to out. You want your brand to transcend that cycle."

While some sociologists had portrayed Gen Xers as listless and cynical slackers, Grasse's business depended on convincing companies otherwise. "Those stereotypes have made me a wealthy man," he added.

On the other hand, a 1997 article in *Brandweek* magazine urged marketers to move beyond the "Gen X label":

> For the sake of effective marketing, the popular perception
> of the skateboarding, bungee jumping, body piercing

slacker must be shed. Somewhere along the way, a dynamic consumer group has become inextricably linked
to a static lifestage...[but] it is absolutely imperative for
marketers to remember that Generation X is not a lifestage; it is a birthgroup ultimately moving through [the]
stages in life.[2]

Evangelicals often are fairly comfortable with the ethos and language of
this secular marketing orientation. A number of churches and evangelical
organizations have largely adopted Madison Avenue's approach toward
marketing Christianity to Generation X. In a sense, that's good, because
evangelical churches and ministries are among the few folks targeting Xers
to give them a message of spiritual hope, not just take their money. On the
other hand, uncritically adopting the marketers' depiction of a generation
may have blinded some churches to the true soul of the emerging generations.

Many thinkers believe it is best to define the generations based on a
combination of time-based and sociological factors. William Strauss and
Neil Howe, authors of acclaimed books like *Generations* (1991) and *13th
Gen: Abort, Retry, Ignore, Fail?* (1993), have developed something they call a
Cohort Group Theory, which takes into account two major components of
a generation's makeup. First, there is a time component, based on the number of years it takes for one generation to grow and reproduce. Second, there
is a "peer personality" component, based on the assumption that members
of a common generation share certain common, defining experiences, even
though they frequently respond to these experiences in unique ways.

Defining a New Generation

Many believe that novelist Douglas Coupland coined the term "Generation X" in his 1991 book *Generation X: Tales for an Accelerated Culture.* But according to author Vann Wesson, an English writer came up with the term and used it as the title for his fictional look at the same 1960s London mod scene that was portrayed by the rock band the Who in Pete Townshend's 1973 rock opera *Quadrophenia.*

For a few years in the late '70s and early '80s, Generation X was the name of the mildly popular English punk rock band fronted by snarling singer Billy Idol, who would later become a best-selling solo artist.

But even if Coupland didn't invent the term, he certainly popularized it and helped give it shape at a time when people were beginning to wonder about the nature of this mysterious emerging generation. He placed his fictional characters—Dag, Claire, and Andy—in a bleak cultural landscape in which a total solar eclipse served as a metaphor for the uncertainties of life. As the narrator says in the book's opening page, he experienced "a mood that I have never really been able to shake completely—a mood of darkness and inevitability and fascination."

Other pop-culture portrayals soon followed. Richard Linklater's pioneering 1991 film *Slacker* cemented the generation's negative reputation, which was further developed in Kevin Smith's 1994 film *Clerks.*

Still, the precise definition of Generation X has remained fluid and open to debate. In the introduction to his 1994 collection *The GenX Reader,* Douglas Rushkoff wrote, "Generation X means a lot of things to a lot of people. We are a culture, a demographic, an outlook, a style, an economy, a scene, a political ideology, an aesthetic, an age, a decade, and a literature."[3]

Mark Saltveit, one of the dozens of young writers featured in Rushkoff's anthology, was less accommodating. "So—what is Gen X?" he asked. "There's no answer, because that's an ignorant boomer question. Who knows? Who cares? Whatever."

A Generation in Crisis

Many people, however, did care, and one of the earliest studies of the emerging generation remains one of the most thorough and detailed. William Strauss and Neil Howe previewed their groundbreaking book *13th Gen* in an article titled "The New Generation Gap," published in the December 1992 issue of the *Atlantic Monthly.*

"In them lies much of the doubt, distress, and endangered dream of late twentieth-century America," they wrote. "As a group they aren't what older people ever wanted but rather what they themselves know they need to be: pragmatic, quick, sharp-eyed, able to step outside themselves and understand how the world really works."

Growing up in a time Howe and Strauss call "the most virulently anti-child period in modern American history," it's no wonder they adopted an "overwhelmingly pessimistic" view of the world.

> They were among the first babies people took pills not to
> have. During the 1967 Summer of Love, they were the
> kindergartners who paid the price for America's new

divorce epidemic. In 1970 they were fourth-graders trying to learn arithmetic amid the chaos of open classrooms and New Math curricula. In 1973 they were the bell-bottomed sixth-graders who got their first real-life civics lesson watching the Watergate hearings on TV. Through the late 1970s they were the teenage mall-hoppers who spawned the Valley Girls and other flagrantly non-Boomer youth trends. In 1979 they were the graduating seniors of Carter-era malaise who registered record-low SAT scores and record-high crime and drug-abuse rates.[4]

In a June 9, 1997, cover story on Generation X in *Time* magazine, a pollster said that idealistic boomer parents left their buster children a difficult legacy: "Divorce. Latchkey kids. Homelessness. Soaring national debt. Bankrupt Social Security. Holes in the ozone layer. Crack. Downsizing and layoffs. Urban deterioration. Gangs. Junk bonds."[5]

Such a legacy left many Xers feeling as if they were a cultural clean-up crew. In addition, many of them seemed constantly worried about what lay in store for them around the next bend in the road of life. "No matter what I plan for the future," one Xer told *Time,* "when I finally get there, it's always something different."

Dealing with Diminished Expectations

In a 1996 lecture titled "Jesus and Generation X," Harvard University theologian Harvey Cox described the emerging generation's "touching disquietude" and "their endearing distress." He observed that this attitude was at least partially influenced by the feeling that earlier generations had left Xers with a world in disarray. As one of the characters in Coupland's *Generation X* put it, "I want to throttle them for blithely handing over the world to us like so much skid-marked underwear."

Andrew Peyton Thomas, an assistant attorney general for the state of Arizona, expressed the frustrations of his generation in the article "Dear Generation X: A Letter to My Cohort," published in a 1996 issue of the *Weekly Standard:* "We will probably be the first generation of Americans that will not do as well as our parents."

A Harris poll conducted that same year reported that half of Xers had trouble sleeping or relaxing because of financial worries. Financial columnist Humberto Cruz put it like this: "We are talking about a world in which young people today will have no assurance they will ever collect social security benefits or be able to hang around with the same company and get a pension at the end of their careers—a world in which they are totally responsible for their own financial well-being."

While some young people recoiled at these prospects and retreated into a series of dead-end "McJobs," others responded with a newfound sense of ambition. A 1997 article in the *American Enterprise* reported that "men and women born between 1961 and 1981 are starting businesses at younger ages and in greater numbers than their predecessors."[6] An article published the same year in the *Harvard Business Review* said business-world busters were taking "a more strictly financial approach to the decisions facing managers," even if that meant doing away with diversity programs or debates about issues like compassion.

Reinventing the Church

This same ambition and zeal that characterized busters in the workplace was evident in the ways that members of this generation sought to reinvent the church. In January 1995, twenty-three-year-old Chris Seay (pronounced "see"), a third-generation Baptist minister, founded University Baptist Church in Waco, Texas. Almost immediately, the congregation became a spiritual home for hundreds of students from nearby Baylor University, many of whom found little of relevance in other Baptist churches. After starting in a small, dilapidated church building, by 1997 the church was meeting in downtown Waco's Hippodrome Theater.

With his short-cropped hair, goatee-style beard, and Sunday-not-go-to-meetin' wardrobe of sneakers, baggy jeans, and plain cotton shirt, Seay's image is a conscious effort to step away from the highly choreographed approach to church championed by congregations like Willow Creek Community Church. "When you coordinate the color of your shirts to the color of your lights, people don't see that as authentic," he told me.

And even though the thought of being a pastor once looked "pretty revolting," Seay eventually felt a calling to reach his generation any way he could. "They're open to the God thing," he said, "but they're not into the church thing."

Seay's early experiments in ecclesiology combined old and new styles. He delivered his sermons from a stool in the middle of a pulpit-less stage, where he would sit down, prop his feet on a nearby speaker, take a sip from a bottle of Snapple, and launch into a meandering monologue about the moral messages in the then-popular R-rated movie *Primal Fear.* Speaking in a laid-back, spontaneous, and self-deprecating style borrowed in part from television's David Letterman, Seay has used the movie's plot of dishonesty and intrigue to bring his audience around to a Socratic inquiry on the nature of truth: whether it can be known, how it can be understood, and where it can be found.

"We can spout Sunday-school answers," he said, "but when it comes to reality, it doesn't really flesh out in our lives."

Hopeful that some in his audience were unchurched, Seay was careful to edit traditional Christian lingo. "Some of you say you don't believe the Bible," he began, "but we'll read it anyway, and see if there's anything interesting in it."

University Baptist served as an important early model for many younger Christian leaders, but it was also a lightning rod for critics such as Thomas Spence, who grilled Seay's approach in a 1997 article in *re:generation quarterly.* Noting that the Waco church's services were a mix of traditional and novel elements, Spence questioned "whether idioms borrowed from the entertainment industry are appropriate for sacred worship." He concluded: "A well-tuned soul naturally recoils from the wholesale invasion of the sacred by the profane."

Like many young leaders, Seay made up his own ecclesiology as he went along, and by 1997 he had plenty of questions about University Baptist himself. By 1999, when his church was attracting around seven hundred people to its Sunday morning services, Seay turned his back on this church and made a pilgrimage to Houston with his wife, Lisa, and daughter, Hanna, to found a church in the city's inner loop. Ecclesia, designed to be a "holistic missional Christian community," held its first official services in January 2000.

Drawing Lines

Emerging Christian leaders like Seay are outpacing the efforts of Christian thinkers, many of whom still are trying to analyze and understand members of Generations X and Y.

Gen Xer Jeff Bantz wrote a sociological analysis of his generation in which he analyzed major implications for churches and mission organizations. A summary of his findings, published in Leadership Network's *Next* newsletter, pointed out some of the tensions and contradictions that bedevil this complex generation. As Bantz put it, Xers

- are very individualistic, but they highly value relationships;
- don't respond to authority, but they long to receive instruction;
- are skeptical yet pragmatic;
- have an extended adolescence, but they grew up too soon;
- are slow to commit but are passionately dedicated;
- are a challenge to manage but are excellent workers;
- are apathetic and yet care deeply;
- are relativistic and searching for meaning;
- are disillusioned, but they are not giving up.[7]

Other thinkers worked to describe Generation X within the context of other generations. George Barna's 1992 work *The Invisible Generation* describes four major generations: seniors (born before 1926), builders (born between 1927 and 1945), boomers (1946–64), and busters (1965–83). Those born after 1983 were "as yet unnamed." Rick and Kathy Hicks's book *Boomers, Xers, and Other Strangers* argues that differences between the generations could be ironed out with a combination of understanding, acceptance, and forgiveness.

27

But it was clear from a 1995 article in *Leadership* journal written by Dieter Zander that some of the major differences between the boomer and buster generations would influence the way they worshiped:

BOOMERS	BUSTERS
"me" generation	"we" generation
live to work	work to live
Jay Leno	David Letterman
enlightenment worldview	postmodern worldview
institutions	relationships
propositional truth	relational truth
excellence	authenticity
growth	community
lonely	alone
success	wholeness[8]

A Ministry Generation Gap?

During much of the last decade, young Christian leaders have been developing a new approach to ministry based on the unique characteristics and needs of Generation X. Writer Andres Tapia described this new approach in an article titled "Reaching the First Post-Christian Generation," published in the September 12, 1994, issue of *Christianity Today* magazine. Wrote Tapia:

> Jesus was in his early thirties when he began his public
> work; he had no career path and no place he could call

home. His greatest battles were against the dogmas of his day, and he showed little faith in institutions and rules and regulations. Rather, his message was of a Father full of grace, and the context of his work was his personal relationships. He built community, first with his small group of 12, and then across class, gender, racial, and lifestyle lines. He liked a good party, even turning water into wine to keep one from ending prematurely. He spoke against injustice and did not have the stomach for inauthentic people. He thought globally but acted locally.

As we confront the growing irrelevance of the church among many Xers, we must wrestle with the idea that Jesus would have felt very much at home with the MTV generation.[9]

At the same time that young leaders have been creating hundreds of Gen X–oriented churches and ministries, others are asking whether an approach to ministry that segments people on the basis of age and other characteristics is really the best way to do church.

In 1999, *re:generation quarterly,* a thoughtful magazine founded to help connect members of Generation X, did a brave thing: It questioned the prevailing orthodoxy of the new ecclesiology. The cover of the magazine proclaimed: "Generation Expired: Rethinking Generationally-Based Ministry." Inside, editor Andy Crouch dared to express the unthinkable:

The segmentation of the American church is dangerous to its health, because the church is not in the business of marketing a product. Segmentation, when not practiced with great care, self-consciousness, and humility, can be fatal, because the real danger of segmentation is that we will forget the gospel....

The church, if it is to be the church, will undo what the marketers have done.[10]

Only during the last few decades have American churches consciously targeted narrowly defined generations, as the seeker-sensitive megachurch movement has done with baby boomers. The strategy has succeeded, if by success one accepts the thinking of marketing executives and measures accomplishment by numbers and the counting of heads.

Are the generation-specific approaches promoted by both boomers and busters expanding the kingdom of God, or are they merely breaking it into bite-sized components? This is one of the major questions that Christian leaders of all generations will be struggling to answer for years to come.

new world–no world

Wrestling with the Implications of Postmodernism

In January 2000, a forty-six-year-old named Ashrita Furman broke a world record by bouncing a mile on a pogo stick in seventeen minutes, forty-five seconds. The feat, conducted at an Argentine military base in Antarctica, was his sixty-second record-breaking feat to be officially recognized by the editors of the *Guinness Book of Records*.

After his pogo-stick performance, Furman told a journalist that he viewed his unusual achievements as spiritual triumphs. "Breaking Guinness records brings me ever closer to my inner truth," said the man, whose previous accomplishments included balancing 57 glasses on his chin for 11 seconds, doing 1,649 squat jumps in an hour, and yodeling continuously for 27 hours.

Welcome to the wild new world of contemporary, post-Christian, postmodern spirituality, where people are busily constructing their own elaborate and highly individualized systems of belief and ritual.

Thinkers vehemently disagree over what—if anything—is meant by the term "postmodernism," a concept first embraced by twentieth-century European intellectuals who were debating subjects like architecture and literary theory. More recently, postmodernism has crossed the Atlantic to America, where in its various forms it has trickled down through the academic disciplines and, with the help of popular culture, become the de facto worldview of the emerging generations.

There is even more heated disagreement about postmodernism's social and cultural implications. But the young men and women who are leading new Christian congregations aren't waiting for an academic verdict on what postmodernism means. They're diving into our turbulent world with a passion to minister in new and sometimes radical ways.

A Generation Meets a Transformation

Down through the ages, just about every new generation has insisted on doing things its own way, believing that its approach represented an improvement on the methods of the older generations. There's nothing unusual about that. But every once in a while, a brash generation comes along at the same time that the world—or parts of it—is undergoing a bold cultural transformation.

Saint Patrick, who Christianized Ireland at a time when Western civilization was beginning to fall apart, later helped inspire the re-Christianization of Europe. Saint Francis, born into the family of a wealthy merchant at a time of unparalleled trade and prosperity, called the church to return to a gospel of poverty and simplicity. And Martin Luther, a devoted disciple of the Roman

Catholic Church, set out to reform Christianity but wound up launching an entirely new movement.

In the twentieth century, young believers were at the forefront of the charismatic movement, the Jesus movement, and the seeker-sensitive church marketing movement. The jury is still out as to whether any of these will someday be remembered as modern-day reformations.

Today, there's a feeling among many members of Generations X and Y that the entire world is shifting beneath their feet and that the older generations just don't get it. And at least some of their elders seem to agree. Peter Drucker, the guru of American management theory, recently rendered this verdict about the contemporary setting:

> Every few hundred years in Western history there occurs a
> sharp transformation. Within a few short decades, society
> rearranges itself—its worldview; its basic values; its social
> and political structure; its arts; its key institutions. Fifty
> years later, there is a new world. And the people born then
> cannot imagine the world in which their grandparents
> lived and into which their own parents were born. We are
> currently living through just such a transformation.[1]

The yearning restlessness and deep sense of purpose, plus the harshly critical stance that many of today's emerging Christian leaders take toward the present-day church, aren't merely the by-products of youthful arrogance, undisciplined exuberance, or too many Starbuck's lattes. Rather, many of them believe they stand at the juncture of two distinct periods of human history. They also believe that unless they radically remake the church, Christian ministry will grow even more irrelevant than it already is.

"Christianity is a generation away from extinction," observed Ken Baugh of the Frontline ministry. "Whether people like it or not, we are the future of the church."

The Definition Is Not the Thing

Mark Driscoll, the bold and outspoken pastor of Seattle's Mars Hill Church, isn't sure postmodernism can be defined, but that doesn't mean he hasn't tried. "Defining postmodernism is a very un-postmodern thing to do," he said. "Categories, definitions, dates, and such feel like impositions forced upon seasons and experiences for the purpose of simplifying and marginalizing things profound."

Ken Baugh agreed. "I don't think you can truly come up with a hard and fast definition of postmodernism," he noted. "In fact, just the question 'What is postmodernism?' is a modern question, because there is the assumption that we can boil it all down into some kind of essence. It's almost like we don't have the right glasses to see it with."

Even though there's little agreement about what it is, there's little doubt that postmodernism is changing our world. Author Jimmy Long called it a "societal hurricane," while theologian Leonard Sweet has written, "The seismic events that have happened in the aftermath of the postmodern earthquake have generated tidal waves that have created a whole new world out there."

Some observers have ventured definitions. Vann Wesson's *Generation X Field Guide and Lexicon* describes it like this:

> Death of the grand narrative, with its beginning, middle, and end. Left without consensus on what comprises good taste or appropriate form, we accept the equivalency of a multiplicity of styles. Las Vegas kitsch competes on the same plane as Wordsworth and a carnival freak show. Postmodern celebrates the fragment: tattoos, film clips, sound bytes, bitstream, and graffiti tags compete with the complete narrative. We freely catapult ourselves into that chaotic sea of information and images.[2]

But the ride, while exciting, can be a bumpy one. As Douglas Rushkoff wrote, "Born into a society where traditional templates have proven themselves quaint at best, and mass-murderous at worst, Busters feel liberated from the constraints of ethical systems, but also somewhat cast adrift."[3]

Others have expressed the essence of postmodernism more succinctly, such as Jefferson Morley, who said, "For us everything seemed normal."[4]

The Postmodern Mission of Mars Hill Church

Many Gen Xers love nothing more than sitting around and debating postmodernism. Mark Driscoll, however, grew impatient with all the talk, and in 1998 he founded Mars Hill Church, which has since given birth to nearly a dozen sister churches. Driscoll believes that God sovereignly placed him in Seattle, the culturally diverse, artistically creative, and robustly post-Christian city he calls home. For Driscoll and other emerging Christian leaders like him, the thing that separates ministry in the twenty-first century from that which went before is postmodernism.

"For me, postmodernism has to be defined in a couple of different ways," Driscoll began. "It includes questions like: What is truth? How do we come to know truth? How do we interpret texts? How do we look at power? How do we look at religion? How do we look at community?

"As it bled into the popular culture and the mainstream, it began to affect the way we do art, the way that we view music, the way that we view style, and the way that we view global issues and being part of an international community.

"That, wed with technology, started to affect people's values, how they view the world, the things that they care about, what they're passionate about, their dreams, their hopes, their fears, the things that they'll give themselves to, and in some ways, their gods and their idols. Postmodernism also has a deep impact on the way that people experience God. It all kinds of bleeds together."

For Driscoll, postmodernism represents the chasm between two irreconcilable ways of understanding the world. "Postmodernism is the death of an old worldview and a transition into a new world where we don't exactly know what will be next. We're in a place of waiting."

But while he's waiting, Driscoll is rolling up his sleeves and extending a hand to people who have known nothing other than a post-Christian, postmodern culture. Unlike some older and more traditional Christian leaders, many of whom see postmodernism and those who embrace it as ideological enemies, Driscoll is trying to build bridges of understanding.

That's why his church is called Mars Hill. "In the book of Acts, Paul starts off his sermon on Mars Hill by saying, 'I see that in every way you are very spiritual.' I believe he meant this as a commendation, a place of beginning. He recognizes that these people had a form of godliness, but they didn't recognize God.

"Like Paul, we have a missional theology that allows us to come into our culture with the full force of the gospel, but we come not to condemn, but to listen."

A Crash Course on Postmodernism

Those who want to research postmodernism's primary sources—and who have plenty of time on their hands—should begin by reading the challenging works by European thinkers Jacques Derrida and Michel Foucault. Those who want to cut to the chase could do no better than reading Stanley Grenz's *A Primer on Postmodernism*. Grenz, a professor of theology at Regent College in Vancouver, British Columbia, has been exploring issues of contemporary philosophy, theology, and ecclesiology for the last decade.

To understand postmodernism, Grenz first examined the modernist worldview that preceded it, springing from the rationalism and humanism of eighteenth-century Enlightenment. "At the intellectual foundation of the Enlightenment project are certain epistemological assumptions," Grenz has written. "Specifically, the modern mind assumes that knowledge is certain, objective, and good. Moreover, moderns assume that, in principle, knowledge is accessible to the human mind."[5]

Postmodernism, on the other hand, is more pessimistic about what humans can truly know. Grenz stated, "Enlightenment realists…assert at least in theory that the human mind can grasp reality as whole and hence that we can devise a true and complete description of the way the world actually works…. Postmodern thinkers no longer find this grand realist ideal tenable…. They argue that we do not simply encounter a world that is 'out there' but rather that we construct the world using concepts we bring into it."[6]

All the tools that modernists used to make sense of their world—including science, language, and even the mind itself—are "deconstructed" by the postmodernists. According to Grenz: "The postmodern understanding of knowledge, therefore, is built on two foundational assumptions: (1) postmoderns view all explanations of reality as constructions that are useful but not objectively true, and (2) postmoderns deny that we have the ability to step outside our constructions of reality."[7]

Along the way, postmoderns also deconstructed Christianity, which over the course of the last few centuries had increasingly adapted itself to Enlightenment rationalism and had come to rely on purely intellectual approaches to everything from biblical interpretation to evangelism.

Brad Cecil, an associate pastor of Pantego Bible Church in Arlington, Texas, where he leads the "aXXess" ministry geared to members of Generations X and Y, described the shift from modernism to postmodernism as "the West's biggest cultural shift in five hundred years." Cecil, who has developed an elaborate time line to describe the transformation, observed, "Before the 1500s, God wrote the story and we were part of it. After 1500, humanity wrote the story, and God was left to write the chapter about faith. Now, there is no unifying story. And people can easily dismiss Christianity, or anything, by saying, 'I'm glad that works for you.'"

Pastor and missiologist Tom Wolf summarized the transition in the following chart:

MODERN WORLD	POSTMODERN WORLD
man is a skeptical person	man is a spiritual person
natural world	embracing alternative authorities
rational authority	re-discovery of the supernatural world
progressive history	disillusionment with historical progress
scientific method	multidimensional methodology
industrial revolution	information revolution[8]

The question that people such as Driscoll, Grenz, Cecil, and Wolf have been asking is, What will become of Christianity as the last vestiges of modernism ebb away? Grenz believes the postmodern period holds both good and bad for followers of Christ: "Christians must not fail…to engage postmodernism critically where that is required. At the same time, they must also be open to what postmodernism can teach us positively as a needed corrective to modernity."

The Dance of Christianity and Culture

It's easy for present-day evangelicals to look back at the worst excesses of the Middle Ages and declare that the Roman Catholic Church sold its soul for worldly wealth and power. But it is nearly impossible for the same evangelicals to see the many ways in which contemporary American values like individualism, capitalism, and consumerism have transformed Christianity in our own day.

Mark Driscoll was raised in an Irish Catholic family in a rough-and-tumble neighborhood before coming to faith during his college years while reading the New Testament alongside works of Greek philosophy and Eastern religion. He has no difficulty detecting traces of secular culture in many of the ways evangelicals have explained and promoted the faith in the twentieth century.

"The 'four spiritual laws' were based on the four scientific laws of Newtonian physics," Driscoll observed. "The emphasis on having a personal relationship with Jesus was developed by boomers who rejected authority, the establishment, and community. Billy Graham, who is a righteous man, talked about 'peace with God.' This approach made sense for people who placed a high value on peace after coming out of two world wars. The gospel really doesn't exist apart from culture."

Driscoll would hope that Christians who are critical of the ways he and other young leaders seek to build bridges with postmodern people would cut him some slack.

"The church has always had these sorts of issues," he noted. "As the gospel goes forth to a new people group, the problem is that the people group that it came from tend to misinterpret the people that it is going to.

"In the first centuries, it was Jews and Gentiles. With Patrick, it was between Romans and Celts. In our present day, it's between moderns and postmoderns. The early church wrestled with questions about whether or not Gentiles needed to be circumcised, or whether they could worship on certain days or eat certain food, and what cultural traditions and customs they could bring with them into the Christian faith. The church is wrestling through those same issues today."

One of the characteristics of postmodernism that evangelicals find most worrisome is its deconstruction of truth claims, but Driscoll isn't caving in on the issue of truth, which Mars Hill affirms as one of its core values: "God is True and revealed His Truth in His Word and the person of Jesus Christ. For this reason, Mars Hill seeks to know, embody, and proclaim Truth out of a love for God and our neighbor."

Still, the church does think postmodern people understand truth in new ways. "People don't find God largely through proposition and through argumentation and defense and rhetoric," observed Driscoll, "but it tends to be in the midst of relationships and community and particular experiences, so worship and experience become huge parts of people's journey to the truth."

Postmodern Poster Boy

Soon after the 1991 publication of Douglas Coupland's debut work of fiction, *Generation X: Tales for an Accelerated Culture,* he became an unofficial international spokesman for the angst and ambivalence of literate, lonely, post–baby boomers. Coupland coined dozens of generational catch phrases, such as "McJob," "veal-fattening pens" (the omnipresent workplace cubicles parodied in Dilbert comic strips), and "air family" ("the false sense of community experienced among coworkers in an office environment"). But people who know little more about Coupland than the fact that he created such sound bites probably don't realize that he has been one of the keenest observers of the spiritual vacuum at the heart of postmodernism.

Whenever Coupland does a reading of his work at a bookstore or other event, fans invariably ask him to sign copies of his 1994 book *Life After God,* which closes with this haunting confession: "My secret is that I need God— that I am sick and can no longer make it alone." And when Coupland wrote in *Generation X,* "You are the first generation raised without religion," he was describing his own thoroughly secular and "insanely middle class" upbringing.

But don't misunderstand him. The same writer who skillfully skewers his generation's skepticism is himself a convinced anti-skeptic. "I am the most uncynical person on earth," he said earnestly. "I'm ironic. I admit that. I'm Joe irony. But people confuse irony with cynicism, which is like battery acid. It just wrecks everything."

And one more thing. Coupland believes in God. "But I'm really mad at him right now," he confessed. "Belief in God is something that's innate in people. Even if you took a group of babies and raised them on a desert island without ever once indoctrinating them about religion, they would probably arrive at monotheism anyway."

In spite of his own religion-free upbringing, Coupland vividly recalls "growing up with this unbelievable sense of yearning for something," a yearning he first tried to express by writing about art.

He remains an unlikely candidate for becoming a card-carrying, church-going believer. "It's like people who were raised without NBA basketball," he noted. "They just don't get what basketball is all about. Look at religion. It's really important to a lot of people, but others just don't get it. My own experience has been like navigating this entirely secular universe, trying to find errors in the system, searching for fault lines where things broke or shifted, looking and seeing what's buried beneath the surface."

One of the reasons Coupland writes so convincingly about postmodern people navigating their way through life is because he is one of them. He even coined the term "me-ism" to describe the beliefs. "Me-ism," he wrote in *Generation X,* is "a search by an individual, in the absence of training in traditional religious tenets, to formulate a personally tailored religion."

Me-ism is a belief system that was explored in the best-selling 1985 book *Habits of the Heart,* except author Robert Bellah called it "Sheilaism."

Sheila Larson was one of the many people Bellah and his team interviewed while researching *Habits of the Heart.* A nurse who had been through a fair amount of counseling, she described the major tenets of Sheilaism: "My faith has carried me a long way. It's Sheilaism. Just my own little voice."[9]

Bellah, who wrote that Sheila's unique faith "suggests the logical possibility of over 220 million American religions," suggested that such ideas represented the move from an earlier type of "public and unified" faith to one that is now "private and diverse."

Spirituality for Sale

Unlike Sheila, not everyone has enough time or creativity to invent his or her own religion. But don't worry, because when postmodernism meets consumerism, there are plenty of ready-made religions available at reasonable rates.

Theologian Harvey Cox observed that Generation X is "the first generation to come of age in a religiously pluralistic America, or at least an America aware of its radical religious pluralism."[10] Theologian Leonard Sweet has written, "For the first time in U.S. history…we are in the midst of a massive spiritual awakening that the Christian church is not leading." And James Hampton, a senior editor for Nazarene Youth International in Kansas City, Missouri, wrote in a January–February 1999 issue of *Youthworker Journal*, "Postmoderns want something bigger than themselves in their lives. They're starving for encounters with the living Christ—and to try Buddha, the New Age movement, and countless other belief systems. It's an all-out, unashamed effort to fill the spiritual void they know exists inside themselves."

Sociologist Wade Clark Roof has done more than anyone to document the rise of a practice called "shopping for faith." In his 1993 book *A Generation of Seekers: The Spiritual Journeys of the Baby Boom Generation* and in 1999's *Spiritual Marketplace: Baby Boomers and the Remaking of American Religion*, Roof and his team interviewed dozens of spiritually hungry boomers.

Roof, who was raised a Methodist, finds a growing discontent with secular "salvations" such as progress, science, or careers and "a yearning for something that transcends a consumption ethic and material definitions of success."[11] Like Lester Burnham, the character played by actor Kevin Spacey in the Academy Award–winning film *American Beauty*, boomers seem to be saying, "I have lost something, but I'm not exactly sure what it is."

Their yearning has given birth to something Roof called "a quest culture,"[12] which is characterized by "a deep hunger for a self-transformation that is both genuine and personally satisfying."[13] For some, this quest has led to church, while others draw inspiration and guidance from books, therapy, self-help groups, the Internet, and popular culture.

"There is a staggering openness to exploring possibilities of belief," wrote Roof, who noted that automakers have christened boomer-targeted vans and SUVs with quasi-spiritual names like Explorer, Voyager, Pathfinder, Discovery, and Odyssey.[14]

"The real story of American religious life in this half-century is the rise of a new sovereign self that defines and sets limits on the very meaning of the divine," wrote Roof.[15]

In a 1999 interview published on the *Salon* Web site, Roof discussed the spiritual yearnings of baby busters, who are the subject of his next book.

"In the minds of many Generation Xers, religion is associated with institutions, organizations, traditional concepts of religion...but the vast majority don't find the traditional language meaningful," he said.

Roof also described our present-day "quest culture," in which people are free to develop their own religions and rituals. In previous generations, young people typically lived their lives in a carefree manner before returning to religious institutions when they got married and had children. But Roof suspects that fewer Xers will return to established churches. "My hunch is there will be a reduced rate of reestablishing institutional religions," he said.

The Promise or the Threat?

Some Christian thinkers such as Gene Edward Veith see postmodernism as, at best, a mixed blessing. "So is the postmodern age good or bad from a

Christian point of view?" he queried in his 1994 book *Postmodern Times.* "Perhaps we will have to say with Dickens, 'It was the best of times; it was the worst of times.'" Ultimately, Veith called Christians to "embrace the opportunities and avoid the traps."

Others are less generous. Stephen Ross, writing in the *Christian Research Journal,* concluded a review of books on postmodernism by warning: "Since central elements of postmodernism, such as its denial of universal truth claims, devastate the biblical worldview, we might wonder whether any association of Christianity with postmodernism hinders the cause of Christ."

But how can emerging Christian leaders disassociate themselves from postmodernism, especially since it is—as one author put it—the water in which they swim?

Like many Xers, Ken Baugh is enthusiastic about the opportunities post-modernism presents. "I think postmodernism is the best thing to happen to the church in two thousand years," he said. "Modernism didn't allow for faith at all, and you can never intellectually prove Christianity 100 percent.

"Postmodernism is a friend of the church because it takes us back to faith being part of the equation."

part 2

emerging values in a time
of transformation

beach bums, latinos, and goths

Subcultures and the Quest for Authenticity

During the 1990s, first-time filmmakers like Richard Linklater and Kevin Smith used charge cards and chutzpa to create passionate and original movies that were among the first pop-culture portraits of an evolving Generation X.

Linklater's *Slacker* (1991) presented more than two dozen unrelated vignettes taken from a day in the so-called lives of the younger residents of Austin, Texas, some of whom could be heard making comments such as, "Same old same old," and "Perhaps human beings weren't made to be happy and free all the time." Along the way, the film not only "defined a new generation," as one movie critic put it, but it also helped popularize a bold new approach to film making that relied on seemingly unconnected narrative snippets instead of one longer metanarrative that tied everything together.

The film opens with a rambling monologue by Linklater—whose character is referred to in the closing credits as "Should have stayed at bus station"—as he takes a cab from the bus station to nowhere in particular. At one point he says, "Every thought you have creates your own reality." The rest of the movie shows the various ways the other characters attempt to create their own realities. One apparently murders his mother before returning to his apartment and the comforts of a religious shrine complete with pictures of Jesus and the pope. Another subscribes to paranoid conspiracy theories. Still another plays in a stardom-starved rock band named the Ultimate Losers. One obsesses over theories about who killed John F. Kennedy, two debate the metaphysics of Saturday morning cartoons, and many try to drink, drug, or sleep themselves into oblivion. Another spends his days watching a dozen flickering TV screens, declaring that "a video image is much more powerful and useful than an actual event."

In 1994, Kevin Smith made his film debut with *Clerks,* a humorous but affectionate look at Generation X as seen through the life of Dante Hicks, who spends most of his life behind the counter at a convenience store in New Jersey. If the setting looks especially lifelike, that's because the film was shot at the same convenience store where Smith himself worked as a youth.

While the characters in *Slacker* seem too overwhelmed by life to make any sense out of it, Hicks and his friend Randal, who works at the video store next door, seem to have given up altogether on ever having meaningful, productive lives—whatever that might mean.

From One Culture to Many

In the years since these films first appeared, scholars began cranking out lengthy academic papers about the characteristics of Generation X and the implications of postmodernism. But for the millions who saw the movies but never read the academic papers, these films had a powerful impact in shaping the world's perception of the next generation.

Today, both *Slacker* and *Clerks* are regarded as cult classics, and both filmmakers have gone on to productive careers in the movies. But people no longer believe that these cinematic portraits tell the whole story of Generation X. If anything, people now pretty much reject the idea that any finite set of characteristics can define an entire generation. Instead, many observers say that Generations X, Y, and those that will come after them are made up of a vast number of smaller, identity-driven subcultures.

America has always had its social, economic, and ethnic distinctions and enclaves, but until recently, many people still subscribed to the myth of a monoculture, believing that America was—or at least could be—"one nation under God." Now, most people see culture not as one but as many.

We could compare this transition to the revolution that transformed the television industry over the last few decades. The old system of broadcast stations and the dominance of a trio of major national networks has been replaced by cable and satellite TV, with their dizzying variety of channel options targeted to every conceivable taste and lifestyle. Likewise, today's kaleidoscope of distinct subcultures is one of the most important differences between the relatively stable social world of the twentieth century and the fluid and fluctuating culture to be inhabited by the emerging generations.

This profusion of distinct subcultures challenges long-cherished ministry models. Gone are the days when churches could be all things to all people by attempting to appeal to the broadest possible audience. Many of today's emerging Christian leaders believe that, in the future, the ecclesiastical land-scape will no longer be dominated by large, monocultural, one-size-fits-all megachurches, but rather by networks of smaller churches, each of which ministers within the context of smaller, more closely knit subcultures.

For many emerging leaders, these notions about subculture are closely related to one of their most deeply held values: authenticity. Pastors who try to be all things to all people, they argue, inevitably come across as phony. Authenticity in ministry, on the other hand, begins with being who you really are and continues by ministering to other people as they really are.

In order to understand what authentic subcultural ministry looks like, let's pay a visit to Evan Lauer, whose church blends relatively seamlessly into the surf subculture of southern California.

California Dreaming

Evan Lauer isn't your typical pastor, and in many ways he's a model for how ministry is happening among emerging Christian leaders who are attempt-ing to do authentic ministry in a postmodern era. Lauer is the founder of Coastlands (www.coastlandschurch.org), an innovative congregation that ministers to members of southern California's sun-and-surf subculture. On many Sunday mornings he rides to Ocean Beach Middle School, where the congregation holds its meetings, on a longboard-style skateboard given to him by one of the many surf-and-skate devotees who attend the church. When the weather is warm (which it almost always is), and when the traffic cooperates (that's a bit less predictable), Lauer can step onto his board in his driveway and coast all the way to church without having to push once.

Once he arrives, Lauer loves hanging out with his church's members, and he's an enthusiastic preacher. "I dig our church," he said.

He's equally excited about his family. "I got to spend the rest of the day and Monday, my day off, with my beautiful wife, Kelly, and coolest kid on the planet, Zach, playing," he wrote in one of his regular, rambling e-mails to his members. "We now have killer weather here and spend the afternoons playing in the backyard while Zach jumps in and out of his kiddie pool naked. During his nap I sat and read the *Surfers Journal* in the shade. I'm one blessed, happy dude. And if that wasn't a good enough weekend, I went surfing this morning with my friend Mike, and we surfed fun waves by ourselves for almost two hours. Just like the song says, I was 'California Dreaming.'"

Lauer is also an amateur drummer, and during one picture-perfect So-Cal Saturday afternoon, he played with a surf-rock band performing at the annual WindanSea Surf Club reunion, held on the beach in scenic La Jolla. "We played everything from 'Brown Eyed Girl' to 'Wooly Bully' to 'Pipeline' and 'Wipeout,'" he boasted in one of his e-mails. "As I played, I watched the people in the water surfing fun, clean 3-4 foot waves. I keep expecting either Gidget, Frankie and Annette, or Elvis to show up. Hey, it's those simple things that get me excited."

Called to Ministry or the Church?

One thing that doesn't excite Lauer is whiling away the hours in a confining church office. In fact, he and many other emerging leaders are wary of the ways in which pastors can be sucked into a swirling vortex of church life and lose touch with the real world. Lauer is doing everything he can to make sure that doesn't happen to him. One of his "second offices" is a portable computer perched on a table in one of Pacific Beach's coffee shops.

"With the advancement of technology," Lauer observed, "I not only have most of my study books either on CD-ROM or my hard drive, but am able to check my messages and receive calls via my handy dandy cell phone. But the best reason to be out in the community is so I can build relationships with people who don't go to our church. If pastors don't watch it, they get stuck in the office all day and never role model exactly what they tell people to do all week, which is to get out there and share your faith.

"So be praying for Monique, who may have me do premarital counseling for her and her fiancé. And pray for the guy (I don't quite have his name yet) and Tara, with whom I'm starting to develop a friendship. Same with a few other people I've met in the last month or so. And by all means, don't get frustrated if you call the church office and I'm not there."

Lauer's involved approach to connecting with the locals is mirrored in the ways some Coastlands members get involved in community activities. Every year the church is one of many groups that rent booth space at the annual Pacific Beach Block Party, which can attract more than fifty thousand people. "I love being there," he said. "Someone walking along sees booths for hemp, bongs, hippie wear, palm reading, and then…a church. Most people look at our sign, shake their head, and keep walking. However, we did have many significant conversations, and hopefully people will come check us out. It's just such a great chance for our church to come to the people instead of expecting them to always come to us."

Church members also participate in the annual Paddle for Clean Water event, which is designed to raise funds and awareness for preserving a clean ocean. And considering its location and culture, the church offers regular surfing classes, attended by members and nonmembers alike.

Occasionally, Lauer's atypical approach to pastoring causes logistical challenges. A newspaper photographer was asking him about props to be used for a photograph that was to accompany an upcoming article about the church.

"Do you have any religious clothes?" asked the cameraman.

"Uh, no."

"Do you have any large religious symbols?"

"Like what?"

"How about a large cross?"

"Sorry."

"Do you have a large Bible?"

"No, just the one I use all the time."

"That'll be fine. Bring that."

Beach Blanket Baptisms

Lauer performs occasional weddings on the sand and baptisms in the surf, but most of his ministerial life is more mundane. And like many young Christian leaders, he seems surprised to find himself presiding over a growing ecclesiastical organization.

"It's getting kinda scary," he wrote in a February 1999 e-mail. The electronic epistle found Lauer musing about the increasing formalization of the church he had founded nearly three years earlier. The formerly seat-of-the-pants group was incorporating and creating bylaws. "I've been doing all these official things regarding our church lately. And this week we'll be having our first official membership meeting."

Lauer also finds himself giving traditional-sounding sermons on topics like financial stewardship or "Why do we need to go to church?" The reasons he cites for fellowship are the ones you would expect (God commands it, it provides us with accountability and fellowship, and we owe it to God); but at the same time, he addresses objections to weekly church attendance with a mix of irreverence and humor, as he did in the following e-mail from August 1999:

> To make it possible for everyone to attend church this Sunday, we are going to have a special "No Excuse Sunday."
>
> Cots will be placed in the foyer for those who say, "Sunday is my only day to sleep in."
>
> There will be a special section with lounge chairs for those who feel that our pews are too hard.
>
> Eye drops will be available for those with tired eyes from watching TV late Saturday night.
>
> We will have steel helmets for those who say, "The roof would cave in if I ever came to church."
>
> Blankets will be furnished for those who think the church is too cold, and fans for those who say it is too hot.
>
> Scorecards will be available for those who wish to list the hypocrites present.

Relatives and friends will be in attendance for those who can't go to church and cook dinner, too.

We will distribute "Stamp Out Stewardship" buttons for those that feel the church is always asking for money.

One section will be devoted to trees and grass for those who like to seek God in nature.

Doctors and nurses will be in attendance for those who plan to be sick on Sunday.

The sanctuary will be decorated with both Christmas poinsettias and Easter lilies for those who never have seen the church without them.

We will provide hearing aids for those who can't hear the preacher and cotton wool for those who think he's too loud!

Hope to see you there!

"We're Not in Kansas Anymore"

You don't have to be a surfer to attend Coastlands, but it might help. At the very least, the congregation isn't for everybody. Which raises the question: Is ministering to narrowly defined subcultures something more churches will be doing in the future? Brad Sargent thinks so.

Sargent, who claims he has a buster's mind in a boomer's body, has made the study of postmodern subcultures a major part of his life's work, and he is surprised more Christians don't do the same.

"Sadly, cultural analysis is not yet a practical skill course required of seminary students," observed the adjunct professor at Golden Gate Seminary in Mill Valley, California, who operates a Web site that distributes some of his studies of emerging ministries (www.ggbts.edu/continuum/unplugged.html).

"Missions-oriented cultural anthropology courses seldom extend their frameworks to contemporary modern or postmodern cultures in the West," Sargent added. "Likewise, courses on youth culture may not address the fact that many contemporary subcultures have historical roots going back fifty years and more and may have worldview roots going back to the nihilist, gothic, romantic, and other subcultures of the nineteenth century."

But even though few people study subcultures, more and more people are realizing how omnipresent they are, how important they are, and how thoroughly they are transforming the ways ministry happens.

"More and more, people realize that we're not in Kansas anymore and never will be again," noted Sargent. "We are now cross-cultural missionaries in our own culture."

In 1996, Ken Baugh of the Frontline ministry at McLean Bible Church in McLean, Virginia, put together a manual called "A Guide to Understanding Generation X Sub-cultures" in which he discussed "extreme" Xers, who get their kicks out of recreational activities like snowboarding; "underground" Xers, whose lives revolve around punk rock bands; "digital" Xers, who prefer cyberspace to the "real" world; "slacker" Xers, who "opt out" of gainful employment and possibly life itself; "super" Xers, who are motivated and career-driven; and "urban" Xers, who live in battle zones and perceive the world as an unsafe place.

But by now it should be obvious that there are many more subcultures, including everything from popular retro-style movements in which young people embrace swing dancing and all its attendant costumes and social mores, and the "lounge" life, complete with its dry martinis and Rat Pack mentality.

And what are we to make of the complex subculture known as "straight edge"? Some of its adherents are devotees of Krishna Consciousness, while others are devout Christians and still others have no specific religious beliefs. But the movement is united by a set of core values, such as vegetarianism, environmentalism, and an opposition to drinking, drugging, smoking, and sleeping around. Many straight-edgers try to promote their views through the music of bands like Prema and Shelter, while others hope their personal examples of disciplined living will persuade others to join their crusade. But some of the more militant Utah-based straight-edgers have relied instead on violence and intimidation. One became a vegan and decided to firebomb a McDonald's restaurant; another repeatedly beats up people with whom he disagrees.

In 1998, Brad Sargent gave a presentation on subcultures at a 1998 Gen X conference in New Mexico. He described dozens of different "identity-oriented subcultures," each of which represents a "personal identity with a specific worldview that is embodied through social identification with a group that holds in common that worldview, typical group behaviors, and 'style.'"

Sargent identified eleven subculture "clusters" that are based on such shared experiences as art, music, fantasy games and exercises; social causes such as environmentalism; extreme or dangerous activities; or sexuality and gender.

Many of these new people groupings represent something Sargent calls

"Transvirtual Urban Tribes." These are interpersonal networks that cut across or transcend national, racial, linguistic, and generational lines. "They are 'transvirtual' in that they are people groups with artificially constructed relationships," he explained, "created primarily by new identity connections based in the age of global information, transportation, and entertainment."

Sargent, who said he feels the closest connection to the cyberpunk subculture, found it baffling that missions experts devote their lives to studying and understanding tribal groups in faraway countries while most believers turn a blind eye to the kaleidoscope of subcultures blossoming in their own country.

"Subcultures will have a lot to do with the probable future look of postpostmodernity emerging in the first quarter of the twenty-first century," he said. "People who want to do incarnational ministry will have to understand subcultures."

Pushing Together

Rudy Carrasco doesn't ride a skateboard to work at Harambee Christian Family Center (www.harambee.org), although he probably could. His ministry's office sits across the street from the house where he lives with his wife, Kafi, and some of the other members of the community. But skateboards are seldom seen in the sometimes-dangerous ten-block urban neighborhood in northwestern Pasadena, where Harambee works with local families.

Even though the Harambee neighborhood is only about 150 miles north of Coastlands' sunny, sandy beaches, the two subcultures these ministries serve couldn't be more different. In the neighborhood Carrasco calls home, more than half the population lives below the poverty line, most of the families are of the single-parent variety, drugs and prostitution are thriving businesses, and a nearby intersection has long been known as "blood corner" because it is where antagonists settle their differences with fists, knives, or guns.

Founded in 1983 by John Perkins, Harambee originally served a neighborhood that was nearly all African American. Today the area is roughly 50 percent black and 50 percent Latino. As a result, the ministry is in a perfect place to observe and understand some of the huge demographic changes sweeping across America as Latinos supplant African Americans as the nation's largest minority group and are well on their way to toppling whites from the privileged majority position they have held for centuries.

"The name 'Harambee' is from a Swahili phrase that means 'let's get together and push,'" said Carrasco, "and what we're trying to do is catch and spread the spirit of working together."

The vast majority of America's parachurch organizations are run by whites, but Harambee is different. Carrasco jointly runs the ministry with Derek Perkins, an African American who is the founder's son. The ministry's logo features a black hand and a white hand locked in a grasp of friendship and cooperation, and that pretty much sums up the philosophy of the ministry's directors.

Racial harmony and reconciliation are top priorities for Rudy and Derek, who, along with their wives, Kafi and Karyn respectively, were cited by *Christianity Today* as four of the fifty leaders under the age of forty to watch in the future. The couples meet with individuals and groups to help mediate racial disputes, and Harambee also sponsors an initiative called

Digital Reconcilers, a Web site offering assistance on reconciliation and community building (www.harambee.org/dr).

Harambee's primary goals are to share the gospel of Christ through evangelism and lifestyle, long-term discipleship of children and young people, service to the local community through "programs and presence," and leadership development.

Stop by the ministry's center on a weekday afternoon and you'll encounter the energy and excitement of dozens of young people participating in Harambee's after-school tutoring program. During the summer, the center operates day camps. And Carrasco, an Internet buff, has given special attention to building up the ministry's computer lab, which addresses the growing "digital divide" separating white kids from just about all others by providing equipment and on-line access. Carrasco even took a group of neighborhood kids on a tour of Silicon Valley. The tour included visits to Stanford University, a stop at the MacWorld Expo Show, and talks with employees of Internet companies like Earthlink, which is a sponsor of Harambee's computer lab.

But even though Carrasco is fascinated by the Internet and the dazzling promises of the electronic future, Harambee spends most of its efforts on the present-day concerns of its neighbors. Every Thanksgiving the ministry is approached by needy families who don't have food for the holidays. "Some families have children in the program, some don't," Carrasco said. "Usually it is difficult for them to ask; they ask in private, off to the side. This year a few of the families we know have had their main breadwinner sidelined by work-related injuries. A few other families were evicted from their apartments and spent more money than they had trying to find a new place. These families and others are already approaching us for assistance."

Harambee also operates an annual Christmas Shop every December 17. "Our Christmas Shop is designed to affirm the dignity of parents and children, so we charge 10 percent of the value of the toy (a twenty-dollar item costs the parent two dollars). Parents hold vouchers that allow them to spend up to a certain amount, and parents receive these vouchers based on points their child earned during the fall program (points are earned for completing homework, good behavior, and attendance). Teenagers are rewarded with gift certificates to places like Ross or Target, because their needs tend to be greater than toys."

Carrasco is a passionate, articulate young man who writes regular columns for the *Pasadena Star News,* the *Whittier Daily News,* and the *San Gabriel Valley Tribune.* If you're interested in finding some of his work, check out www.urbanonramps.com/rc.

He has a strong sense of his overlapping identities as a Hispanic American, a member of Generation X, and a servant of Christ. And he doesn't see his ministry as being directed at a subculture. But he acknowledges that urban people have a unique culture and unique needs. He and other urban ministers, including Saji Oommen in Fresno, David Benavides in Santa Ana, and Kevin McCloskey in San Diego, regularly meet together and sponsor forums to inspire and train others interested in serving the city.

These young urban ministers, members of the national Christian Community Development Association, even believe that their form of service is one of the best ways to think globally but act locally by living out their faith commitments in ways that make a positive difference for the people around them.

Paint It Black

On April 20, 1999, two high-school students walked into Columbine High School near Denver and opened fire on their classmates and teachers. When the shooting ended, twelve students and one teacher lay dead. Afterward much of America lost some of its optimism and innocence as it pondered the ramifications of this deadliest high-school shooting in the nation's history.

In the days and weeks following the event, reporters began to probe into the lives of the two killers in an effort to uncover a hidden motive. These investigations brought to light the fact that large schools like Columbine contain small, hidden pockets of sometimes pathologically oriented young people who feel alienated from most of their fellow students but find some solace in alternative subcultures. In the case of the Columbine killers, their own minigroup, called the Trench Coat Mafia, had at least some connections to the Goth subculture, many of whose members dress in black clothing, wear dark makeup, and listen to musically harsh and lyrically nihilistic rock music.

Most Americans had never heard of this youth subculture before Columbine, but some committed Christians were already seeking ways to reach out to this troubled and isolated tribe.

As the son of disgraced television evangelist Jim Bakker, Jay Bakker had gone from living in the warm glow of the celebrity spotlight to experiencing a humiliating public disgrace. The night his father was sentenced to prison, Jay began a journey into alcohol, drugs, and despair. By age twenty, Jay was getting help from Alcoholics Anonymous, a group that exhibited the type of redemptive grace he believed churches should have. And over the next few years, he founded a handful of ministries around the country designed to show that kind of grace to alienated members of the Goth subculture.

Bakker, who founded his first outreach in Phoenix, called his ministry Revolution. By 1997, he had moved to southern California to live with his father and establish a Los Angeles version of the ministry. By 1999, Jay and his wife, Amanda, were in Atlanta, where their work in reaching out to young outcasts got the attention of a writer with *Rolling Stone.*

"The church should be there for people," Jay told the writer. "Because Jesus sat with the scum. He sat with the sinners and prostitutes. I don't know how we've gotten so out of touch."

Meanwhile a pastor named David Hart was doing the same kind of work in San Diego with a ministry called Sanctuary (www.pobox.com/~sanctuary).

"Our official mission is 'to Reach the Marilyn Manson Generation for Christ,'" Hart said. "We are here for anyone seeking sanctuary and searching for answers in a dark world."

The group has its main meeting on Sunday afternoons, and there are additional Bible studies throughout the week, as well as a regular on-line ministry directed both to church regulars and members of the international Goth underground. During late 1999 and early 2000, Hart led a Bible study series on the book of Nehemiah and taught a class examining the spiritual implications of the popular movie *The Matrix.* Members of the congregation also went as a group to a movie theater to watch the Oscar-nominated film *The Green Mile.*

Hart is passionate about his ministry, but he is also aware that members of the subculture to which he ministers harbor deep animosity toward organized religion. Therefore, when Sanctuary began holding its Sunday afternoon gatherings at San Diego's Scott Memorial Church, Hart felt he needed to tell his young adherents that he wasn't compromising his deepest values.

"Have no fear," he wrote in one of Sanctuary's on-line newsletters, "we are not being conformed or compromised by the church. Sanctuary is still not what most people expect. We continue to be an outreach to the misfits and the castaways of Generation X, Generation Y, the Marilyn Manson generation, the Gothic subculture, the Industrial nation, hard-core kids."

Neither Jew nor Greek?

At a 1998 national gathering of Gen X pastors, one young man whose congregation has been reaching out to vampire-oriented members of the Goth subculture barely caused a stir when he told a group of his fellow ministers, "We invite these kids to share Communion with us, and it gives them a whole different understanding of blood."

In recent years there has been a flowering of ministry to subcultures. In Ventura, California, the Reverend Ryan Delameter hosts weekly gatherings of skateboarders at a local center named Skate City. Kids who usually pay twelve dollars to skate get in for free if they're willing to listen to Delameter preach about Jesus.

Throughout the country, nearly one hundred members of the Christian Tattoo Association reach out to the tattoo, body-ornamentation, and scarification subcultures by creating dazzling designs on people's skin.

And in the San Francisco Bay area, the Prodigal Project reaches out to disaffected young people who have migrated to the city's fabled Haight-Ashbury district by offering them food, free showers, Bible study, and for those who are serious about walking with Jesus, discipleship at a former bed-and-breakfast in Mendocino County.

Examples like these could be multiplied by the hundreds, and for many people, these kinds of incarnational ministries represent the cutting edge of Christian outreach.

But others aren't so sure. Brad Sargent believes subcultural ministry is essential, but he also warns of its potential pitfalls.

"If we go with the missiological 'homogenous unit principle,' where we basically mingle only with the same kind of people as we are, I believe the underlying 'hidden curriculum' message is one of racism, classism, subculturism, and etceterism," Sargent said. "A church contextualized for a particular subculture where the church barricades itself off from other Christians or the world relationally is unhealthy."

While we should thank God for the men and women who are doing subcultural ministry with people who have been ignored or marginalized by the mainstream church, their work also raises questions about growing divisions in the body of Christ. What, for example, would the apostle Paul make of it all? What would subcultural ministry look like to the man who told the Galatian believers, "There is neither Jew nor Greek, slave nor free, male nor female, for you are all one in Christ Jesus" (3:28)?

Many of today's emerging leaders take an approach that focuses on ministry to the generations and subcultures they feel have been largely ignored by the mainstream church. And even though most of these leaders affirm their belief in the unity of the body of Christ, some of their ministries seem destined to widen the divisions in that body, not heal them.

desperately seeking soul mates

The Comforts and Challenges of Community

When French historian and politician Alexis de Tocqueville came to the United States to do research for his groundbreaking study *Democracy in America* (1835–39), he was so intrigued by the country's unique national character that he had to coin a new term to describe it: "individualism."

In the 1990s, President Bill Clinton reaffirmed the national commitment to empowering Americans to think, decide, and vote for themselves, declaring, "In America to be an individual is our highest value."

But during the last few decades, many observers of the American scene have raised troubling questions about our growing addiction to notions of individualism and the self and about the negative impact this addiction can have on family, civic society, and the church. As Robert Banks wrote in *The Complete Book of Everyday Christianity:*

Throughout the West our undue stress on the individual
is fragmenting family life, diminishing our sense of friendship, isolating neighbors from one another, making the
workplace increasingly competitive, involving us in court
cases more often, reducing our involvement in civic
affairs, diminishing our interest in politics and making
religion a private matter.[1]

Novelist Douglas Coupland, who has chronicled Generation X's desperate attempts to find hope and meaning, has repeatedly written about the
emerging generation's rejection of individualism and its growing hunger for
community and friendship. In *Generation X,* he described one character's
near-obsessive search for some kind of meaningful connection: "All looks
with strangers became the unspoken question, 'Are you the stranger who
will rescue me?' Starved for affection, terrified of abandonment, I began to
wonder if sex was really just an excuse to look deeply into another human
being's eyes."

Other characters used a variety of creative ruses to disguise their unful-
filled hopes for connection, some by hanging out with members of their "air
family" (which Coupland defined as "the false sense of community experienced among coworkers in an office environment"), while others gave
expression to their "terminal wanderlust" (which expressed their "hopes of
finding an idealized sense of community in the next location").

Sociologist Wade Clark Roof confirmed such concerns in his 1999
book *Spiritual Marketplace: Baby Boomers and the Remaking of American
Religion.* Roof wrote that in their quest for meaningful spiritual lives, many
boomers want to be grounded in a community of shared spiritual values,

but at the same time they want to remain fluid and unencumbered. "There is," noted Roof, "the dilemma of wanting social support and community, yet resisting too much infringement on personal space."

Thankfully, there is ample evidence that many of the emerging post-boomer leaders are placing a priority on community, which they believe is the only antidote to the aloneness and alienation many of them have experienced in their families and the larger society.

"A new type of family, one that is composed of friends, is being established today," wrote Jimmy Long in *Generating Hope*.[2] Long argued that community is a major part of a new postmodern paradigm. He observed that the premodern period (up to A.D. 1500) was best summarized by Anselm's statement, "I believe in order that I may understand." The modern period (1500–1960) was captured by Descartes: "I think, therefore I am."[3]

"If the postmodern era has a catchphrase," noted Long, "it may be 'I belong, therefore I am.'"

Long, like many other Christian thinkers and writers, believes the emerging generations' commitment to community may be one of the most praiseworthy elements of their evolving ecclesiology. "We should be embracing this change because tribalism, or community, is much more closely aligned than the autonomous self to God's intention of how we should function in relationships," he wrote. "God created us to live in community."[4]

Still, talking about community and creating it are two different things, and there are indications that the brokenness and alienation that many young people have experienced makes them more hungry for community but also may make them less able to create and sustain it. With that in mind, it is helpful to examine the ancient and modern roots of our problems with community, as well as explore some of the new groups that are seeking a solution.

Postmodern Dreams, Modern Buildings

In Coupland's 1999 novel *Miss Wyoming*, a former beauty queen emerges unscathed from a deadly airplane crash and wanders into a pristine and life-less suburban scene. "The neighborhood seemed to have been air-freighted in from the Fox lot, specifically designed for people who didn't want community."

Ron Johnson, pastor of Denver's Pathways Church, feels the same way about many of the buildings that he and other emerging Christian leaders have inherited from their boomer predecessors. Boomers, after all, built megachurches, with row after row of forward-facing seats designed more for spectators than participants.

In late 1999, Johnson was elated that Pathways could begin meeting in a small, inner-city Methodist church where the pews were arranged in a circle, enabling members to see and interact with one another. For years the church had been meeting in a large classroom building at the University of Denver. While the facility was relatively inexpensive to rent and also helped the church reach out to college students, Johnson was never very happy with the place.

"That room, with its stage and rows of theater seats, was against everything we stood for," commented Johnson, who founded Pathways (www.pathwayschurch.org) in 1995.

In addition to its layout, the room presented other problems. Church volunteers had to spend hours every Sunday morning loading and unloading the materials and equipment they used to help transform the educational hall into a sacred space. Although they dimmed the room's bright lights, decorated the stage with dozens of large candles, and projected images of medieval icons on a large screen behind the stage, the room remained cold and uncomfortable.

"There were also way too many entrances and exits," said Johnson. "It makes it hard to get people involved." In order to get people to come earlier, Pathways offered a variety of coffees, teas, and juices before the service. And in an effort to get them to hang around after the service, the church offered beverages and half a dozen varieties of bagels and toppings. On some Sundays, young people would linger for an hour or more, eating and talking.

Still, the space never felt like a community area. On some winter mornings, the room was so cold that Johnson could see his breath as he gave his sermon. On other mornings, volunteers had to clean up beer bottles and remnants of hashish brownies left in the back of the room following a Saturday night party on campus.

But even during their sojourn in the university wilderness, Johnson and other Pathways members strove to build a sense of community within their congregation. The church sponsored small groups for men, women, married couples, and "mixed" constituencies. In addition, member Matt Tuley organized a movie group called Masterwing Theater. On Sunday nights, dozens of church members and their unchurched friends would gather at a member's house to view a classic film and dine on barbecued chicken hot wings.

In their efforts to help members of the buster generation become passionate, devoted followers of Christ, leaders of new churches have tried all kinds of approaches to combat individualism and create community. In the process, many of them have come to believe they are ushering in a radical new reformation of church life.

The Way Things Were Supposed to Be

According to the young theologians of Generations X and Y, people were created to enjoy community. They flourish when they experience it, and they shrivel when they don't. One might think, then, that people would make creating and enjoying community one of their top priorities in life. But over the millennia, obstacles as ancient as the Fall and as new as the Internet have conspired to make deep and lasting community difficult to achieve.

Still, according to an increasingly prevalent attitude within emerging Christian circles, community is at the heart of the way things were supposed to be in the cosmos. In the beginning, eons before there was anything else, there was God. But God was not a solitary individual, for there was community and interdependence among the three persons of the Trinity: Father, Son, and Holy Spirit. These three persons worked together in creating humanity, saying in Genesis 1:26, "Let us make man in our image."

For a while, the man and woman God created enjoyed communion with each other and with their Creator. But then sin, selfishness, and self-protection entered the picture. Adam and Eve ate the forbidden fruit, sought to blame others for their sin, and became awakened to their own nakedness.

God kicked Adam and Eve out of his garden paradise, but he didn't give up on them. In time, God sought to redeem humanity through the nation of Israel. During much of this time, he remained a somewhat elusive figure who revealed his will through his commandments but couldn't be approached directly by any but a select few human representatives.

Christ and Radical Christian Community

With the incarnation of Christ, God was no longer aloof and mysterious but could be approached, touched, and loved. During his brief earthly ministry, all anyone needed who wanted to know what God was like was to look upon Jesus.

Following his crucifixion, resurrection, and ascension, people could no longer look at Jesus, but they could experience his ongoing presence and redeeming love in the midst of the community found in his mystical body, the church. As we learn from the second chapter of the book of Acts:

> They devoted themselves to the apostles' teaching and to
> the fellowship, to the breaking of bread and to prayer.
> Everyone was filled with awe, and many wonders and
> miraculous signs were done by the apostles. All the believ-
> ers were together and had everything in common. Selling
> their possessions and goods, they gave to anyone as he had

need. Every day they continued to meet together in the temple courts. They broke bread in their homes and ate together with glad and sincere hearts, praising God and enjoying the favor of all the people. And the Lord added to their number daily those who were being saved. (2:42-47)

Two chapters later, these radical followers of Christ continue to place the demands of community above the temptations of selfishness.

All the believers were one in heart and mind. No one claimed that any of his possessions was his own, but they shared everything they had. With great power the apostles continued to testify to the resurrection of the Lord Jesus, and much grace was upon them all. There were no needy persons among them. For from time to time those who owned lands or houses sold them, brought the money from the sales and put it at the apostles' feet, and it was distributed to anyone as he had need. (4:32-35)

But as with the Garden of Eden, a serpent of selfishness was loose in the church. The purity and passionate commitment to community was tested by Ananias and Sapphira, who, we are told in Acts 5, sold some property and deliberately withheld some of the money for themselves.

The man was confronted by the apostle Peter. "Ananias, how is it that Satan has so filled your heart that you have lied to the Holy Spirit and have kept for yourself some of the money you received for the land?... What made you think of doing such a thing? You have not lied to men but to God" (5:3-4).

With that, Ananias fell down and died, to be joined a short time later by his wife. "Great fear seized the whole church and all who heard about these events" (5:11).

For a time, anyone who wanted to know what God was like could have looked at the church, where his divine character was on daily display in all the mundane details of life. But the selfishness of Ananias and Sapphira demonstrated that sin also was at work. And in succeeding centuries, the unity of the mystical body of Christ would be challenged, both from without (by persecution) and from within (by division and the lust for earthly power and worldly wealth).

The Ascent of the Individual

Over the past twenty centuries, older ideas about community have been challenged by newer concepts of the autonomy of the individual. Although a commitment to the dignity of every person is an idea with plentiful biblical support, there is growing evidence that our single-minded commitment to individualism has robbed us of the joys of community. The Protestant Reformation, for example, with its insistence that individuals could read and interpret the Bible on their own, upset centuries-old systems of spiritual and ecclesiastical authority. The European Enlightenment only gave further credence to the idea of the autonomous self. Then the industrial revolution, which emphasized efficiency above all else, led to the destruction of traditional craft guilds and the creation of urban centers that, even though they teemed with people, seemed to make community harder to come by.

American expressions of the Christian religion, from the time of the Great Awakening to today's mass evangelism rallies, have emphasized personal, individual conversions to Christ much more than they have stressed the importance of creating communities of faith. And in the 1980s and 1990s, the seeker-sensitive church movement placed increasing emphasis on appealing to the perceived needs of fickle, autonomous religious consumers, downplaying the very real "costs" of discipleship and ignoring the biblical call to radical Christian community. George Barna, in *Marketing the Church* (the bible of the seeker-sensitive movement), boldly challenged Christian leaders: "Think of your church not as a religious meeting place, but as a service agency—an entity that exists to satisfy people's needs."

Making Connections

Many emerging leaders reject the anticommunity ecclesiology of most boomer churches, and if they are successful at creating a sustainable alternative, the twenty-first century may provide the church with a more fertile ground for the building of deeper Christian communities.

If you hang around with young pastors or attend conferences where the discussion centers on ministering to Generations X and Y, you are likely to hear angry critiques of many of America's largest and most "successful" churches. In the eyes of many emerging leaders, these churches funnel thousands of people into big, impersonal, auditorium-style facilities to sit in individual theater seats to listen to a highly polished, high-decibel worship music team that makes the audience's participation unnecessary. After hearing a brief, well-crafted sermon that focuses on their perceived emotional needs, the crowd quickly files out of the auditorium, in some cases very quickly, to make room for the next group preparing to file in and repeat the whole impersonal process all over again.

But an ability to be critical of the boomer paradigm isn't in itself a guarantee that the emerging generations will be able to improve things. And some thinkers have argued that members of the emerging generations may actually be psychologically incapable of achieving true community.

William Mahedy, who has served as a college chaplain and young adult pastor for the Episcopal Church in San Diego, and Janet Bernardi, the coordinator of campus ministries for the same church body, are the coauthors of *A Generation Alone: Xers Making a Place in the World* (1994). In their chapter "The Healing Community," Bernardi argued that, because of the emotional traumas many Xers have been through, they "suffer symptoms similar to those of post-traumatic stress."[5] Mahedy added that large numbers of Xers are afflicted with a variety of other clinical disorders, including borderline personality disorder, identity disorder, problems with self-image, pervasive fears of abandonment, and a "pervasive pattern of instability."[6]

Even so, Mahedy is hopeful that Christian community can be a healing and redemptive oasis for these suffering people. "In a culture like ours, where the individual is dehumanized," he wrote, "the recovery of genuine humanity begins with the forming of real friendships. Friends genuinely care for one another."[7]

While some young Christian leaders seem to be approaching the issue of community with both eyes open, others seem content to merely pay lip service to the idea. In the years ahead, these differing approaches to community will have a huge impact on the future shape and impact of the church.

Connecting Through Sex

Busters were born into a sex-saturated mass media society that has no precedent in world history. Authors Glenn Gaslin and Rick Porter discuss the impact of sexually explicit entertainment in their *Complete Cross-Referenced Guide to the Baby Buster Generation's Collective Unconscious* (1998). Young people grew up hearing news reports about Ted Bundy, the "serial killer who…got to know his victims before he brutally raped and murdered them." They could also hear Bundy immortalized in a song by Jane's Addiction called "Ted, Just Admit It."

Dr. Ruth Westheimer dispensed explicit sexual advice in books, magazines, and over the radio and television. And if Dr. Ruth's material sounded too clinical, kids could listen to raw material in hits by "boy toy" Madonna ("Like a Virgin"), Meatloaf's epic ballad of drive-in lust ("Paradise by the Dashboard Light"), and 2 Live Crew's shocking lyrics (which could be heard on the album *Nasty As They Wanna Be* or in congressional testimony on the harmful effects of rock lyrics).

Increasingly, movies dealt with sexual topics, but it wasn't always fun to watch. For every lighthearted teen movie like *Dirty Dancing,* there was a shocking film like *Fatal Attraction,* in which a one-night stand results in obsessive stalking and an attempted murder. For every fancy-free *Flashdance* or *Footloose,* there was another one of the frightening *Friday the 13th* sequels, in which characters have sex and then get hacked to death with a lawn-mower blade.

When an estimated thirty urban punks bludgeoned and raped a woman jogging through Central Park, the press dubbed the act "wilding" and people talked about "how bored, violent, and degenerate the youth of today have become."

During the 1980s and '90s, condoms became omnipresent but so were a variety of sexually transmitted diseases, the most deadly of which was AIDS. And during the '90s, movies like *Go* (which, according to one reviewer, showed young Los Angelinos as "wolfish and hungry, up for anything that will make them feel alive") and hit songs like Bush's "Chemicals Between Us" or the Goo Goo Dolls' "Iris" expressed a generation's need for relationships as well as its deep sexual ambiguities.

Joshua Harris, a young Christian author, represented part of a conservative backlash against America's pervasive sexual libertarianism. His book *I Kissed Dating Goodbye,* which advocated a return to traditional rituals of courtship, sold hundreds of thousands of copies. But most kids were tuning into popular television shows like "Friends," the mega-popular sitcom about the lives and loves of six busters who would frequently engage in dialogue like this:

Joey: "When I first met you, you know what I said to Chandler? I said, 'Excellent butt, great rack.'"

Phoebe: "Really? That's so sweet. I mean, I'm officially offended, but it's sweet."

Sex Mis-Education

When Eric Konigsberg investigated the sexual habits of today's college students for *Spin* magazine, he found out a lot more than he bargained for. Konigsberg asked one male student and one female student at Vassar College to keep journals of their sexual exploits during a fourteen-week school semester. The writer also talked to other students about their sex lives. The resulting magazine article read like some hedonistic nightmare.

"Having reached the point of nearly complete license, they had created an environment that seemed melancholy, nihilistic, groping, purposeless, apathetic, lifeless," read the article, which was published in 1998 and titled "Sex Ed."

The students interviewed for the article had as few hang-ups about opening their lives to the writer as they did opening their beds to their fellow students. The male who kept a journal for the story recorded sexual encounters with ten people—not quite one partner per week. The female recorded a more conservative three partners.

In addition, other students told stories about "pseudo-orgies" (in which they hang out in a dorm room, drink, and get gradually naked), about students propositioning each other in the school's dining hall, and about the yawning chasm that has opened up between copulation and love.

No one talked about falling madly in love or about getting hurt, wrote Konigsberg. "No one fought to save a romance, and no one worked to start one." Instead, much of the emphasis was on bedding and being bedded, even when sex was a seeming afterthought. "When they did end up in bed, it seemed to have been just that—ending up there by chance, or due to someone else's insistence."

Walt Mueller is the president of the Center for Parent/Youth Understanding in Elizabethtown, Pennsylvania. Mueller regularly immerses himself in pop culture, so he wasn't particularly surprised by the *Spin* article. "I've heard this all before," he said, "over and over. Should we be surprised by these behaviors in a young adult population that longs for connectedness and has been raised largely by media messages that promote free expression of sexuality?"

And while some may question the article's anecdotal approach or even *Spin*'s agenda (its editor is the son of *Penthouse* publisher Bob Guccione), Mueller doesn't think we should dismiss the message because of the messenger. "While the article may not accurately reflect the sexual reality of 100 percent of today's college student population, it is at least an accurate portrayal of how some are living."

Mueller said some of the article's findings are confirmed by his own conversations with youth workers and high-school students. One youth ministry veteran told him that kids "are so much more sexual in the way they dress, talk, and behave. And they feel the freedom to be so much more sexual in front of adults. They don't even try to hide it." As for high-school students, Mueller has found that while not all are "doing it," most are feeling a growing freedom to "talk about it." These signs of increasing sexual frankness represent the practical consequences of society's growing sexual permissiveness and the media's growing explicitness.

While some who read the *Spin* article may want to bury their heads, Mueller said the article made him more excited about the prospects for youth ministry today. "The article reflects the gnawing emptiness, search for meaning, and purposelessness in our culture," he observed. "Students are looking to connect with themselves, with others, and with God in significant ways."

Fast and Easy at High School

According to "The Lost Children of Rockdale County," a shocking documentary aired in 1999 as part of the PBS *Frontline* series, sexual openness is trickling down into younger age groups. The documentary examined afflu-ent Conyers, Georgia, a quiet Atlanta suburb where a 1996 syphilis outbreak infected 17 residents and forced another 250 to get medical treatment. Most surprising was the fact that the outbreak affected young people, some as young as twelve.

A few of those affected reportedly had had as many as one hundred sex-ual partners, and others said they regularly attended sex parties where young people would pair off or gather in groups for quick liaisons, sometimes watching the Playboy channel on cable television and mimicking the behav-iors they saw.

In the documentary, which is one of the most powerful depictions of contemporary teenage angst ever produced, boys talk openly about their sexual conquests, girls discuss honestly their disappointment about their erotic activities, and parents say they had no idea what their children were doing, adding that they wouldn't have known what to do about it even if they had known.

Meanwhile, things weren't going much better in Arlington, Virginia, a wealthy suburb near the Washington, D.C., beltway. Officials at Williams-burg Middle School invited parents to a meeting about teenagers who, eager to avoid pregnancy, were regularly engaging in oral sex. Most of the teens seemed to believe that oral sex was less "intimate" or significant than inter-course, and many seemed to think this type of promiscuity was a way to pre-serve their virginity.

"It's now the expected behavior," said a school district health official, according to *Washington Post* reporter Laura Sessions Stepp, who wrote about the incidents in a July 8, 1999, story.

Most often, according to Stepp, kids would engage in oral sex at parties or in parks. There were also incidents in much more public settings, including one in a crowded eighth-grade study hall and another on a school bus on its way back from a seventh-grade field trip. One enterprising Reston boy even attempted to make money by helping classmates connect before being convicted of solicitation and sent to a juvenile detention center.

Most of the Virginia teens engaged in oral sex as a way of trying to find either pleasure, fulfillment, or a sense of affection that they didn't receive from their parents. As could be predicted, these sexual liaisons seldom produced the desired results. One young girl who hoped sexual activity would help her snare a desired boyfriend was disappointed. "I realized pretty soon that it didn't make him like me," she told Stepp.[8]

Voices in the Wilderness

The 1992 film *Singles* provided a lighthearted look at the baby buster generation "in search of itself" through relationships, most of which were portrayed as unfulfilling and frustrating. As for sex? "Casual sex doesn't even exist any more," says one character in the film. "It's lethal. It's over."

It's clear that many young people are looking for an alternative to sexuality as they have known it in the past. Still, churches seeking to minister to sexually adventurous Gen Xers and Yers will be required to help these young people redefine lost distinctions between moral and immoral behavior, even if their defense of sexual sanity sounds like a voice in a promiscuous wilderness.

Here are some of the current efforts:

1. Instill Hope

Many churches focus on Bible stories about men, but increasingly they must give girls hope through Bible stories describing women. "The Bible is full of stories about wonderful women like Ruth, Esther, Deborah, the woman at the well, the hemorrhaging woman, the Proverbs 31 woman, and the Virgin Mary," said one young leader. "These are stories of courage, commitment, and hope."

2. Rebuild Self-Esteem

Many young people connect through sex because they aren't aware of other ways to achieve personal peace or community. One of the ways many leaders are trying to help is by involving younger people in leadership, including such things as asking them to lead the group in prayer or to teach a Bible study.

3. Practice Affirmation with Women

"We need to take a look at the ways we affirm girls," said one leader. "Too often, we compliment them on having a cute skirt, pretty hair, or nice behavior. We don't affirm their insights or their activities as often as we should, whether it is their sports activities, their academic achievement, or other gifts they may have."

4. Be Prophetic

Young leaders need to talk clearly and openly about God's design for sex without being vague or coy. Instead, they should attempt to talk about sexuality as frankly as kids do themselves and as clearly as do the movies and TV shows they watch. But at the same time, they have to include the important missing elements in so many discussions about sex: God's high view of humanity and sexuality's important role in fostering communication and intimacy between men and women.

5. Preach Purity

Leaders need to help young people develop practical strategies for maintaining sexual purity. That requires more than merely reciting lists of sexual dos and don'ts. Instead, help young people see through the sexual lies and empty promises of today's culture and create a stronger, deeper set of personal values. Young people need to see the benefits of biblical sexual morality, not just the prohibitions.

6. Proclaim Redemption

Living a life of sexual purity has never been easy. Leaders will encounter a growing number of believers who are "sexual casualties." The challenge is to lead them to faith, forgiveness, and a new sense of wholeness. With the right approach, Christian leaders can help restore young people to a healthy, biblical approach to sexuality.

beyond proposition

Experiencing God in Worship

Plenty of Christian organizations exist primarily to engage in commerce, such as marketing books and CDs or selling tickets to concerts and lecture tours. But rather than merely marketing merchandise, a relatively new organization called Passion (www.PassionNow.org) organizes events that attract thousands of young people. Founder Louie Giglio identified the ministry's main purpose: to bring young people together to help them experience God.

"God is moving in fresh ways throughout the world," he noted. "It's the 'wind of the Spirit' Jesus refers to in John 3. The student culture seems more primed to be blown by that spiritual wind because they are not tied to forms, but more open to a full-on mind, body, and spirit connection with Christ. There is a hunger and a driving thirst for an experiential faith—one based in truth yet experienced on all levels of life."

Events sponsored by Passion feature Giglio and other speakers, along with a topnotch worship band that leads people in singing songs like Matt

Redman's "Did You Feel the Mountains Tremble" and "I've Found Jesus" by England's Delirious? But unlike traditional youth events that focus primarily on stirring young people's emotions and challenging their minds, Passion moves on to an important next step by helping young people have spiritual encounters with the living God.

Here's how Giglio, an animated speaker whose excitement about the Christian life is evident, opened the group's Passion '99 conference, which drew eleven thousand students to the Fort Worth Convention Center: "We want you to know that you haven't come to an event, but you have come to meet with the living God. We have not come here to celebrate people. We have not come here to gather around a theme or the name of a conference. We've not come here to celebrate any other name but the name of Jesus Christ."

Founded in 1997, Passion has focused on glorifying God and encouraging young people to do the same. In May 2000, the group brought tens of thousands of young people to its One Day conference in Memphis (www.OneDay2000.org).

"The picture of the gathering is the picture of a generation of students lying on their faces before God," Giglio said. "For one solid day, we're going to be before God."

Evangelical youth groups haven't necessarily been known as centers of mystical devotion, but many of the college-age students attending Passion events appear to be experiencing something that medieval saints would have considered spiritual ecstasy. While singing songs that express deep spiritual yearning and choruses like "Better Is One Day in Your Courts Than Thousands Elsewhere" or "Pour Down Your Spirit Like a Shower," thousands of young people clapped their hands and raised their arms toward heaven.

Some even closed their eyes and swayed slightly as they sang "Be Glorified," a song Giglio cowrote.

Perhaps there's nothing too unusual about that, but some of these young people knelt on the floor, lost in silent reveries. Some shouted and screamed with exuberance, while others simply stood silently. Tears of joy and cleansing could be seen trickling down their faces.

Asked about their experiences, the young people testified to the fact that Passion's goal of helping people pursue intimacy with God has been achieved. "The Holy Spirit was just speaking to me about worship," one said. "To me, everything in my life is an opportunity to meet him," commented another. A third announced, "The main thing God has been teaching me is that it ain't about me, it's about him."

Giglio says the experiences of young people like these is evidence of the existence of something he calls "a 268 generation," a reference to Isaiah 26:8: "Yes, LORD, walking in the way of your laws, we wait for you; your name and renown are the desire of our hearts."

A Hunger to Experience God

Some people see Passion and related ministries as parts of a larger movement that is taking younger Christians beyond proposition to experience.

It was writer Douglas Coupland who, in his book *Life After God,* had one of his characters say, "In spite of everything that has happened in my life, I have never lost the sensation of always being on the brink of some magic revelation." Sentiments like these led writer William Mahedy to comment, "Xers are, I believe, at least potentially a 'sacramental generation.'"

Henry Blackaby, whose book *Experiencing God* became a runaway best-seller, said the common factor among many unrelated contemporary movements is people's hunger "not to know more about God, but to experience God. Not to know more information, but to have a transformational personal encounter with God."

Blackaby, a veteran pastor, said he wrote *Experiencing God* because many people asked him for guidance on moving beyond thought to relationship—a process that hasn't always been taught in Christian churches. As he told the on-line publication *Leadership Network Explorer,*

> The heart of the Christian life, whether it's in the workplace or in the church, is to have that personal, intimate relationship with the Lord. That was the heart-cry and there was nothing out there that was even coming close to touching it.
>
> I didn't write it because I knew there was a vacuum; I did it because I was asked to. I have seen the hunger in the hearts of God's people for the reality of a relationship with God that makes a difference. Not, "How can I use God to make me successful?" but "How can I be involved with what God is up to?"

Blackaby said he has seen this hunger in many places, including corporate boardrooms. But one of the places it is felt most strongly is among older teens and young adults.

> We have a generation of youth that are as serious as any generation I've ever seen for God to use them. In conferences that I lead, usually four or five of them will come up

to me and say, "We want you to know we feel the generation that preceded us or the leaders who guided us
betrayed us, and our nation is in an awful condition.
We're meeting every morning of the week to pray, believing that maybe it is our generation that God will use to
bring revival to America."

These aren't kids who want to be entertained or who
are looking for success. These are kids who are very serious
about believing that their lives can make a spiritual difference in their nation and touch their world.... They may
not be able to clearly identify it, but they know that those
who have gone before have left the nation in an awful mess,
and they feel that God is calling them to make a qualitative
difference in their nation. This generation is determined to
let the world know who Christ is through their lives.[1]

Involving the Whole Person

Christians have long spoken about the importance of having a relationship
with God, but too often God has been reduced to a series of theological
propositions. Instead of having a genuine relationship with God, many
people have subsisted on a rational understanding only.

Sally Morgenthaler, an author, speaker, and workshop leader who is sort
of a roving ambassador of vital worship, said it took her a while to realize she
had spent much of her life merely paying lip service to connecting with God.

"I said I had a personal relationship with God, but what I meant was that I had thought through everything, and it seemed logical to me. I had gone through the 'four steps' to salvation, but I had not let God into my life, or into my personal story, or into my pain. We can get so operational and didactic about this thing we call 'having a relationship with Jesus Christ' that we don't even realize we're not having a relationship."

Unfortunately, just as individuals can mistake thinking about God for really knowing him personally, churches can substitute times of professionally performed and emotionally moving singing for times of real worship. The fact that the church bulletin says "Time of Worship," or that the musicians providing the instrumental accompaniment are called "a worship band," doesn't guarantee that worship is taking place. For Morgenthaler and others like her, the changing ways in which the emerging generations of believers are worshiping God is another powerful indication that the West is undergoing a transformation.

From Science to Mystery

"The world that I grew up in was a world without God," Morgenthaler observed. "We went to church, but God was dead, and instead we worshiped science. With science, we went to the moon, we developed weapons that were unheard of, and we developed computer technology. Growing up at a time when so many of these things were nascent, we worshiped science. We went to church on Sundays, but the rest of the week we went to school and we worshiped science.

"In that kind of world, we didn't really think about experiencing God. Instead, you went to church and you got the manual. I think that's why a lot of us were out of there as fast as we could go when we were older, because we really did want to experience God, but we couldn't seem to do it at church. I went to church, and I was told all the right things to do and think, and I got theology—but I didn't get God.

"But over the last fifteen years, there's been a move toward an approach to God that is experiential instead of just thinking about God," Morgenthaler continued. "To be postmodern in many ways means that you are open to spiritual things, and that you are seeking spiritual things. Today we live in a world where people are supernaturalists, and the younger you are, the more that is the case. Now we are in a world where to be an atheist is a very uncool thing. Movies like *The Sixth Sense* and TV shows like *Roswell* are full of a sense of experiencing God.

"People have understood finally that *they're* not it, that human beings are not the sum total of life, and that there's got to be something else out there. The postmodern world is one where we are fascinated with the mystery of it all."

Seekers and Finders

Ironically, mystery is something that most celebrated baby-boomer church leaders have systematically removed from their services. At Willow Creek Community Church, the flagship of the seeker-sensitive movement, services are designed to appeal to the aesthetic tastes of someone senior pastor Bill Hybels calls "unchurched Harry." Willow Creek's services are as devoid of religious trappings as the church's walls are of explicitly Christian symbols such as crosses.

But pastors like Todd Hahn of Warehouse 242 in Charlotte, North

Carolina, say the busters are different. They aren't turned off by spirituality or mystery.

"That would be one area where we differ from more traditional models, or even contemporary models like the seeker model, which has influenced us a lot," Hahn remarked. "We love what God has done in those movements, but that's not what we're called to do.

"We believe that for postmodern people, the distinction between seeker and believer in terms of religious experience is less than it has been for previous generations.

"What we are about is creating a worshiping community that is radically hospitable. We try to hit both those things by being an authentically worshiping community, so that our service is not a performance, and it is not particularly outreach, but it is real worship. At the same time, it is radically hospitable."

Hahn and other emerging leaders think Sally Morgenthaler got it right in her 1995 book *Worship Evangelism: Inviting Unbelievers into the Presence of God.* The book argues that instead of dumbing down worship services for people who aren't Christians, churches should invite unbelievers into their periods of mystical worship, praying that they will experience something of the presence of God while they are there.

"Church is a place where we are supposed to be able to meet God, but often we don't meet God there," commented Morgenthaler. "Young people want to encounter the 'other' at church, but they are not finding it there. They're finding programs, they're finding games, they're finding cute things to do, but they're not finding an experience with the other they assume is there somewhere in the world.

"But just because they don't find it at church doesn't mean they're going to stop their search. They're going to find it somewhere, and it's the church that is missing out."

Young leaders like Hahn and Morgenthaler still care about reaching seekers, but they don't think the best way to do that is by producing choreographed, spiritless worship services that rarely go deeper than the superficial aspects of life.

"We are all seekers," Morgenthaler observed, "except for many people in the church who have stopped seeking any kind of mystery, or a God who is bigger than they are. I think people are having some of their most spiritual moments going to the movies, or watching Oprah. God isn't dead any more. God is back, but sporting a lot of costumes. And churches are just the Judeo-Christian dish in the smorgasbord. And understandably, we're not the first thing people go for."

Blending Old and New

Leonard Sweet has said, "Postmodern leaders are visionaries spellbound by the past." Not surprisingly, one of the ways many postmoderns learn about worshiping God is by studying premodern ways of worship practiced by everyone from Ireland's ancient Celtic Christian monks to the twentieth-century French brothers from Taize (pronounced "tezz-ay"), whose rituals incorporate elements of Gregorian chant and lengthy periods of silence and prayer.

"The Holy Spirit seems to be working new convictions in the church, particularly among members of the younger evangelical generation who differ significantly from the older generation of Christians," wrote Robert Webber, the former Wheaton College professor who now teaches at Chicago's Northern Baptist Theological Seminary and serves as the director of the Institute for Worship Studies.

In his 1999 book *Ancient-Future Faith: Rethinking Evangelicalism for a Postmodern World,* Webber determined that many young people are looking to the distant Christian past for spiritual guidance: "The older generation is attracted to the details of theological systems, tends to think in exclusive either/or terms, enjoys debates over theological points, tends to be passive about social issues, and wants to maintain the status quo. They have been shaped by the science, philosophy, and communication theory of the modern worldview. Therefore, they opt for security and stability over change."

But the newer generation has been shaped by a different set of values, and younger believers feel a powerful attraction to ancient spiritual traditions. "The early tradition of the faith dealt with basic issues," Webber noted, "and was concerned with unity, open and dynamic, mystical, relational, visual, and tangible." As he observed, "Thus the primary reason to return to the Christian tradition is because it is truth that has the power to speak to a postmodern world. Early Christian teaching is simple and uncluttered, it cuts through the complexities of culturized Christianity and allows what is primary and essential to surface."

In practice, Webber favors neither a full-fledged return to the hymns of earlier centuries or a wholesale embrace of new forms of worship. Rather, he prefers a blended approach that uses the best elements of both. "In the twenty-first century," he said, "we will see a convergence of trends that draws from the early church with its mystery, transcendence, and the Eucharist; from the Reformation, with its centrality of the Word; from evangelicalism, with its central emphasis on Christ and strong singing; and from the contemporary church, with its emphasis on intimacy and relationships."[2]

Excavating Older Traditions

In a March 1, 2000, article for Religion News Service, journalist Peter Smith described the growing worldwide popularity of liturgical forms developed by the Protestant brothers of Taize, a phenomenon Smith witnessed firsthand at a church in Providence, Rhode Island.

"A group of casually dressed young adults prayed silently, sitting cross-legged on floor cushions in a chapel beneath the city's Episcopal cathedral," Smith wrote.

> Dozens of votive candles sent deep, glimmering reflections onto the tile floor. Softly, the participants' voices gathered into a chant:
> "Stay with me, Lord Jesus Christ, night will soon fall.
> "Stay with me, Lord Jesus Christ, light in our darkness."
> They repeated the verses ten times, perhaps twenty or thirty. One by one, worshipers came up to a large icon of a cross laid flat in the center of the chapel. Each spent a few moments of prayer there, some kneeling upright and others resting their foreheads on the cross. Such is the essence of Taize liturgy, a style of worship steeped in some of the most traditional religious trappings—candles, incense, icons, chants—yet holding an enduring appeal for the young and, often, unchurched.

Although few Gen X churches follow such a specific form of worship, many congregations are increasingly incorporating older liturgical elements, along with visual trappings like candles and icons, that are designed to set a mood for encountering the mystery of God.

Mark Yaconneli, the Gen X son of author, speaker, and Youth Specialties founder Mike Yaconneli, has long been singing the praises of something he calls "ancient-future youth ministry," which he has described in magazines like the *Christian Century* and *Group*.

"A youth program is effective only when it offers kids the space, tools, and time to encounter God's transforming love," Yaconneli wrote. He contends that a contemplative approach to youth ministry based on ancient spiritual traditions is a superior alternative to programs based on either entertainment and activities, a charismatic youth leader, or propositional instruction.

Is It Pop or Is It Praise?

For most of the first centuries of Christianity in America, believers who gathered to worship would sing songs contained in psalters and hymnals or learned at church music conferences or crusades. This traditional approach to worship music persisted until the 1970s, when the Jesus movement and the charismatic movement introduced more contemporary styles, as well as new approaches to composing and distributing praise choruses.

In 1974, Calvary Chapel's Maranatha! Music label released its groundbreaking debut, *The Praise Album*, which featured melodic, memorable songs like Karen Lafferty's "Seek Ye First," still one of the most popular praise choruses in America. By mixing lyrics of praise with music influenced by mainstream folk, pop, and rock genres, the new worship music obliterated the traditional barriers between church music and consumer entertainment, helping to meet a growing hunger for experiencing God by producing and marketing praise music people listened to at home or in the car.

The Jesus movement and the charismatic movement also took church music out of the hands of degreed and credentialed professionals and turned it over to spirited, pop-oriented laypeople. Today the praise and worship music industry funnels music both to church musicians and consumers through a growing number of record labels, dozens of praise- and worship-oriented radio stations, periodicals, conferences, and informal networks.

Record labels like Integrity, Vineyard, and Worship Together are taking new worship music to an audience that probably constitutes the American church's first post-hymn generation. The most successful praise and worship company is Integrity, Inc., a publicly traded corporation founded in 1987, which had $35 million in sales in 1998 to become the nation's second most successful Christian recording company. The company's mission is "helping people worldwide experience the manifest presence of God," something it has attempted to do through its popular Hosanna series—now ninety albums strong—which creates and markets live recordings of churches at worship.

"We don't sit around with fifteen writers and think about cool songs we're going to feed to the church," noted Danny McGuffey, Integrity's senior vice president and general manager. "We find songs that are being sung in churches all over the world and harvest those songs."

The Vineyard Music Group, affiliated with the Association of Vineyard Churches, also disseminates songs and choruses that already are being sung in churches in America and around the world.

"Our priority is songs that come out of the Vineyard movement—songs that we believe have been given to us by God—and taking them to the world at large," said Alex MacDougall, the label's general manager. MacDougall played drums with Daniel Amos in the 1970s, was a Maranatha! executive through much of the 1980s, and took the helm of Vineyard's label in early 1998 after the deaths of movement founder John Wimber, who had formerly been a successful secular musician, and Wimber's oldest son, Chris.

MacDougall stressed that Vineyard songs are "written *to* God, as opposed to *about* God," and are characterized by their I-and-thou orientation. "Good praise and worship music has been tremendously beneficial to the church," he noted. "Folks who for whatever reason resisted singing the hymns have embraced these songs, which help them experience worship that is intimate and at a deeper level."

Worship Music for the Masses

Praise and worship music companies like these have drastically changed the way Christian music is sung and disseminated. But even though millions of believers may be singing some of the same songs and choruses, there's no uniformity of musical style, commented John Styll, publisher of the fifty-thousand-circulation *Worship Leader* magazine. "You can have a pretty straight-laced but theologically liberal Presbyterian church using the same songs that are being sung at a wild and crazy charismatic church, but they use different arrangements and adapt the songs to their unique settings."

Worship Leader also publishes *SongDISCovery*, a bimonthly worship resource featuring a CD of recorded music and an accompanying songbook that gives thousands of subscribers a sampling of new praise and worship music. The service allows worship leaders to tailor worship music to each congregation's style and taste.

Gen X–oriented music companies like Worship Together have used the Internet to distribute new worship music. More than twelve thousand worship leaders regularly download songs at www.worshiptogether.com, the label's Web site.

Quality or Quantity

But does the ever-growing quantity of worship music necessarily improve the quality of believers' worship experience? Apparently not. A survey conducted by George Barna found that less than one-third of adults who attend church services feel as if they have truly interacted with God.

John Witvliet, director of the Calvin Institute of Christian Worship at Calvin College, expressed concern that contemporary worship music has inherited more than hip musical styles and topnotch recording techniques. He said it also has blindly swallowed pop music's overemphasis on celebrityism and performance, turning worship leaders into prima donnas and turning congregations into passive observers rather than active participants in the experience of worship.

"One potential downside to all the music being distributed via high-tech distribution is that it may tend to be more performance-oriented rather than congregational," Witvliet observed. "Most of it is recorded with soloists or a small band rather than with or for assemblies of people. Perfect high-tech recordings can be discouraging to faithful musicians in small churches without the means to produce such a perfect sound."

Turning Concert Halls into Churches

Worship music has become big business, but at the same time, some of the most popular Christian-label recording artists have made worship music a regular part of their albums and concerts.

Bands like Jars of Clay include praise-oriented songs like "Love Song for a Savior" on their best-selling releases. Jars joined supergroup dc Talk and other artists on last year's popular *Exodus* album, which featured praise songs by a dozen artists. One can also buy ska-influenced praise music by The Insyderz, or Code of Ethics' album *Blaze,* which features Euro-pop renditions of popular praise songs and carries this consumer warning: "Repeated exposure...may cause the listener to be brought closer to God who is a consuming fire."

But no band has done more to bring mystical experiences to concert audiences than Delirious? (www.delirious.net), a British band that participated in a huge Christian concert at London's Wembley Stadium that attracted an estimated forty-five thousand young people in 1996.

In 1992 singer Martin Smith and some of his friends started a small youth group called Cutting Edge at the Arun Community Church in Little-hampton. The church is a nondenominational charismatic congregation, one of many grass-roots fellowships popping up in a country where most believers are at least nominally affiliated with the Church of England.

The Cutting Edge meetings, which were held once a month on Sunday nights, featured teaching, worship, and Smith's catchy, original worship music. Over time the band's renown began to spread, and Delirious? began recording some of its music, which was first released in the United States in 1997.

The band is among the many musicians who are sparking a spiritual renewal among youthful Britons. "What is happening, especially among young people, is that they're just being woken up and falling in love with Jesus and being passionate, and not being frightened or ashamed to make it known," observed band member Stuart Garrard.

"I think we've helped to make worship a cool thing, if I can say it like that," Garrard added. "People haven't been afraid to bring their non-Christian friends along to a worship gig. I think that's something we've pioneered, along with people like Matt Redman. We make music the kids can feel like they can worship to with freedom and abandonment.

"Especially in the early days, what we were really going for was a whole sort of abandonment in worship, which was a challenge, especially amongst a generation that is trying to be cool all the time. Instead, we've tried to say, 'let's be fools.'"

Garrard believes his band's music is only effective because the band members' constantly strive to listen to God and invite him to empower and use their music.

"When people talk to us, and ask us, 'What are your aims? What do you want to do with the band?' We say we totally want to play the best music we can. We believe we can be one of the best bands in the world. At the same time, we want to see the presence of God come wherever we go. God is up to something, and if we can play a small part in that, that will be fantastic."

A Revival of the Arts

In many new churches, it's not just music that is being used to worship God. The visual arts are being celebrated as well.

Steve Taylor is a musician and visual artist who founded Squint Entertainment, a company best known for recordings from bands like Sixpence None the Richer, Waterdeep, and Burlap to Cashmere. Taylor believes the best way to get through to nonbelievers is through the work of "artists who are passionately committed to Christ, and passionately committed to excellence."

"Gen X is this nation's first post-Christian generation," remarked Taylor. "It's not that they haven't heard the gospel. They think they know what Christianity is, and they don't want any. So how do you get the attention of people who don't want to listen? I believe two of the best ways are modern music and film."

Protestants have had an uneasy relationship with the visual arts ever since iconoclastic Protestant reformers destroyed icons and statues in the name of God. In the centuries after the Reformation, the church, which for centuries had been a patron of the arts, grew increasingly distant from them.

Some emerging leaders are trying to change that by encouraging young artists, featuring art in their services and buildings, and holding gatherings at art galleries. But in doing so, they're fighting against centuries of Protestant assumptions about how words are deemed important to God but visual beauty is treated as irrelevant.

"One of the things that frustrates me the most about living in the Christian community is that it seems I have to cut off part of myself to live there," commented author and speaker Sally Morgenthaler. "Our lives seem aesthetically narrow, like we can only use three primary colors. But I would like to have the whole box of crayons and call it good."

For the new generations, the whole box of crayons might be just the beginning.

chapter 6

God deconstructed

Proclaiming the Gospel in Postmodern Times

For much of the last half of the twentieth century, most people who wanted to be pastors went to seminaries, where they took courses in Bible, theology, counseling, and preaching. The courses in preaching often were under the heading of "homiletics," and in these classes, students would study the rhetorical methods developed by ancient Greek philosophers and orators, by Bible patriarchs and evangelists and well-known preachers. But rarely would any of these students be required to spend any time understanding the ways people "hear" information in a postmodern world influenced by an approach to literary analysis known as deconstruction.

"Deconstruction," wrote Jimmy Long, "is the uncentering of modern life that leaves us with multiple possibilities and the equal validity of all interpretations." MTV, Long suggested, is a perfect symbol of deconstructionism, with its ever-changing visual images reinforcing the idea that "there is no grand theme to life."

Changes in worldview and philosophy transform the ways people receive and process information, and veteran preacher and storyteller Calvin Miller has observed that Christians who want to communicate effectively must spend time studying how present-day people hear.

"It should be more about how people listen than how preachers preach," Miller told Leadership Network's *NetFax*.

> Preaching ought to be determined by how people listen, and so I talk about things like making the "communicator's promise." Every night, newscaster Peter Jennings tells me what he is going to tell me in the next thirty minutes. Preachers need to be up front with people about why they are getting together and what the sermon is going to be about.
>
> This is a day and age when you really need to think about and study to whom you are speaking. The hardest work I do is always audience analysis—trying to look at those people and figure out who they are before I am in front of them. In my books I call it the "speech before the speech."[1]

While some seminaries have paid little attention to how people hear, *Trial*, a magazine for trial attorneys, devoted space to the subject in its July 1997 issue in an article called "A New Generation of Jurors?" Author Noelle C. Nelson, a trial consultant, argued that lawyers need to be aware of the fact that Gen Xers who serve on juries hold values and attitudes that may make the attorney's job more difficult. Among Nelson's points:

- "When debriefing the jury, [an attorney] often finds that the younger jurors were not only bored by his presentation but they also found no real meaning in his case."
- "I have found that Xers generally view experts as 'hired guns' who are credible only if they can demonstrate their objectivity."
- "Many members of Generation X have little faith that the law reflects what is 'right.' What matters most to them appears to be whether an action is fundamentally 'wrong,' not whether it is legally defined as a crime."
- "Generation X jurors assumed the plaintiff was well-off simply because he was fifty years old and appeared dignified.... Not surprisingly, the Generation X jurors voted against compensating the plaintiff because of what they perceived as his privileged economic position."
- "Attorneys should use clear and simple language, speak in short phrases, and pause frequently. They shouldn't lecture."

A similar case was made in the March-April 1997 issue of *The Futurist:*

- "Xers hate anything that is hype and smacks of phoniness."
- "They want their information concrete, concise, and to the point."[2]

The Power of Stories

When Jesus wanted to describe the mysteries of the kingdom of God to the people who were following him, he often wrapped his lessons in stories. He communicated complex and potentially confusing ideas—profound ideas about the nature of God and his relationship to the human race—in the most basic and simple of stories. Think of the immediately comprehensible tales about the sower, the talents, the mustard seed, the prodigal son, the good Samaritan, the wheat and the tares, and dozens more. Jesus' parables captured people's imagination and were told and retold for decades before being written down in the New Testament Gospels.

But over the next nineteen centuries, many preachers and teachers lost the art of telling such stories, particularly during the post-Enlightenment "modern" era, during which most preachers seemed bent on doing away with stories altogether and instead bombarded their listeners with sermons full of lists, teaching points, and practical proposals.

One exception has been in African-American churches, where preachers and congregations delight in the telling of long, colorful yarns. But for much of the twentieth century, most white churches were virtual story-free zones. Of course, there were illustrations aplenty, but few real, vibrant stories. Sermons in the twenty-first century will be much different if members of Generations X and Y have anything to say about it.

Seeing Life As a Story

Author Douglas Coupland wrote eloquently of the power of stories in *Generation X.* Claire, one of the book's characters, argues that life is more than a succession of isolated moments. "Either our lives become stories, or there's just no way to get through them."

If anything has become clear about the emerging generations of Christian leaders in the decade since Coupland wrote those words, it is that they are returning to the lure and power of stories.

Sure, many Christians continue to treat the gospel message as if it were primarily a set of rational propositions about God, or a series of therapeutic techniques, or even a body of "evidence that demands a verdict." But the emerging pastors and leaders widely disregard such approaches.

Stories are flourishing in postmodern preaching, both stories from the Bible and stories from people's lives. And pro-story preachers cite a number of reasons for adopting this approach, including the fact that stories communicate effectively in a visually oriented, postmodern age that lacks an overarching metanarrative.

As one young leader put it at a 1998 conference, "If you are presenting Christianity as a list of dos and don'ts or as a set of rational propositions, people can critique your presuppositions, or question your motives, or just dismiss you altogether. But if you tell stories—either Jesus' or your own—it's easier to make connections."

That's because of the ways unique stories work, said Brian McLaren, an author and the senior pastor of Cedar Ridge Community Church in Burtonsville, Maryland, who spoke about stories at a 1998 conference. "A story doesn't grab you by the lapels and bring you close so that you can smell the cigarettes and coffee and Altoids on his breath. What a story does is sneak up behind you and whisper something in your ear. And when you turn around to see what it is, it kicks you in the butt and runs and hides behind a bush. And in so doing, a story does something that no abstract proposition can ever do. It stops you in your tracks and forces you to think. It catches your attention and won't let you go. You can't help it.

"A story can't be argued with or dismissed like a proposition," he continued. "A story is just sneaky. It doesn't teach by induction or deduction. It teaches by abduction. It abducts your attention and won't let you go until you have done some thinking for yourself."

McLaren, a baby boomer who is a frequent speaker at Gen X events, doesn't think it's an accident that Jesus used stories in his own ministry of teaching and preaching. As he sees it, Jesus was the incarnation of God, and Jesus' stories were the incarnation of the gospel message.

"The story is the point," McLaren asserted. "Why drain it of its blood, skin it, stuff it, mount it, and present it as an outline of abstractions and limp moralisms the way I so often have done? C. S. Lewis understood this, which is why so many of us love him. Narnia can teach you more about hope and heaven and Jesus than a boxed set of my best sermons, including the fill-in-the-blank outlines."

Not everyone is a born storyteller, but people can learn. McLaren believes they'd better start doing so—and quick.

"Telling The Story is best accomplished through the use of stories," he contended, "but they are not the same thing. An effective pastor today must be a teller of The Story, the great biblical, Genesis-to-Revelation Story, not just a good storyteller. The challenge for those communicating in the emerging culture is to use the wonderful benefits of storytelling to tell The Story to a culture that is looking for a context of 'when and where' for the many questions of 'what and why.'"

A Fresh Look at the Biblical Story

There are more stories and other literary materials in the Bible than there are straightforward doctrinal lessons, but during most of the twentieth century, preachers and teachers downplayed the role of story and turned Bible lessons into expositions of cold, hard facts.

"Frequently, the Bible is viewed as merely a sourcebook for doctrine, a guidebook of maxims for successful living, a manifesto for making public policy pronouncements, or a stick with which to beat others who are not like ourselves," wrote Todd Hahn and David Verhaagen in their book *Reckless Hope.*[3]

The people at the International Bible Society have been hanging out with Gen X leaders for the past five years. And as they have listened to the ways young preachers talk about the Bible, they have been rethinking its relevance for a postmodern era.

"Gen X was raised on TV, movies, and videos," observed Michaela Dodd, a product manager at IBS and a member of Generation X, "and our church services reflect what we know.

"One pastor at a Gen X conference in Orlando said that he felt uncomfortable with the way many churches used Scripture. He said the type of sermon he grew up hearing was like a pyramid. You start with Scripture and build your sermon on it. He felt that the words 'Open your Bible...' were alienating to a generation who may not own a Bible and wouldn't know how to read one."

But as the speaker continued, Dodd wasn't sure his approach to remedying this problem was much of an improvement.

"This pastor preferred starting off with humor or a story that everyone could relate to and then eventually getting to Scripture at the end. He compared the opening of his sermons to David Letterman's shtick at the beginning of the TV show *Late Night*. He thought the best thing you could get your audience to do was to laugh, applaud, or cry. He said when he thought about the emotional level he wanted his congregation to be at, he thought of a Disney cartoon. He thought this offered a good example of tone—seriousness interspersed with comedy and building to a climax."

Dodd was frustrated that the pastor advocated resorting to sentimental—and possibly manipulative—approaches to "warm people up" to the Bible. "If a sermon's emotive capability is preplanned," she remarked, "it threatens authenticity, a value highly held by Gen Xers."

She has attended plenty of Gen X conferences and heard plenty of sessions on worship, teaching, evangelism, and church structure, but she said she's heard little creative thinking about the Bible. According to Dodd, "Most buster churches seem to treat the Bible the same way as the boomer church I attend. One exception is Mark Driscoll of Mars Hill Church in Seattle. He is passionate about the Bible, and he's been able to build a successful church with many people who have caught his passion for Scripture."

The International Bible Society has been trying some creative new approaches in the ways it packages and presents biblical texts. At a Gen X conference in 1998, representatives of IBS led a session on the Bible in which they invited young leaders to share whatever came to mind when they thought of the Bible.

"Foreign and negative," said one leader. "A book of recommendations," said another. "Legalistic, a book that is used as a weapon," said a third.

IBS has been trying to reformulate the way it packages the Bible, and the first fruit of this new thinking is The Wisdom Chronicles, a series of CD-sized booklets that are presented as "a series of books bringing you time-tested, perennial wisdom."

The booklets include portions of various Bible books but don't proclaim the text in a way that will turn off people who think they know what the Bible is all about or have already determined that they don't need it.

Book One, *Practical Words of Insight and Understanding,* is "compiled from the ancient Middle Eastern book of Proverbs." Like the other books, it dispenses with the traditional chapter and verse numbers, treating the text like a "normal" book. Book Two, *Pondering the Meaning of Life,* is "compiled from the ancient Middle Eastern book of Ecclesiastes." Book Three, *Piercing the Mystery of Suffering,* includes excerpts from Job, while Book Four, *The Sayings of Jesus,* is "compiled from the collections of Jesus' sayings that were written closest to the time that Jesus actually lived."

It's too soon to tell how popular these booklets will become, and IBS officials never think they will outsell the ministry's popular sports Bibles or other products geared for churches and chaplains. Still, the effort indicates that some new leaders are trying to find creative ways to introduce new audiences to the wisdom of the Bible.

A Fresh Look at Preaching

Most of us have experienced something like this: When a church service begins, people are smiling and animated as they let their voices rise in songs of praise to God. Depending on the church, some stand while others kneel; some raise their hands to the heavens while others bow their heads; some smile with joy while others weep tears of release.

But then a change comes over the crowd. After a period of active participation, the faces of a multitude of worshipers suddenly glaze over with blank, drowsy stares. Men and women who moments before were vibrant during the praise portion of the service fall into a stupor. The reason? The pastor has stood up to deliver the sermon and participation time is over. It's the preacher's show now.

Most preachers—no matter what their age—preach as if they are involved in a monologue: they are the presenters, and the job of the congregation is to listen. Thankfully, some creative new approaches stress the important of incorporating interactive elements into sermons and other presentations.

"The challenge for pastors is more than just dispensing wisdom in a half-hour time frame, but to teach in an interactive fashion that captivates the listener, much as Jesus did," wrote Sundee Frazier in the November-December 1998 issue of *Worship Leader* magazine. Frazier said preachers could introduce interaction in three ways: by encouraging interaction between people, encouraging interaction with God, and giving multiple options for response.

"No two of us are alike," she wrote, "and the way we respond to poignant preaching will likewise differ. By permitting people to respond in a way that reflects their gifts, temperament, and level of spiritual maturity, we allow individuals to act on the lessons they have learned, rather than giving them reasons to justify their inactivity."[4]

Kelly Williams is the twenty-nine-year-old pastor of Vanguard, a Gen X church he founded in Colorado Springs in 1997. Up to two hundred people attend Vanguard's Sunday morning and evening services, which employ creative and even controversial approaches to communicate Christianity to a generation that thinks it already knows what it is and has rejected it. During a sermon on the crucifixion of Christ, for example, Williams steered clear of sentimental church art and instead played clips from the film *Braveheart,* which features Mel Gibson as William Wallace, who gave his life to liberate the Scottish people.

A series on end-time scenarios from the book of Revelation was illustrated by some of the congregation's musicians, who gave a polished, high-decibel performance of "Enema," an apocalyptic song by the hard rock group Tool.

And a sermon about hell featured clips of Pinhead, the evil star of the gory *Hellraiser* films, which have been condemned by many other churches.

Williams's training is about as traditional as it can get. He is a graduate of Jerry Falwell's Liberty University and of Dallas Theological Seminary. His church is affiliated with the Southern Baptist Convention. And there are times during his sermons when, if you close your eyes and pretend you are in a traditional church, you can picture Williams as an old-time Bible thumper. He loves expositional preaching.

But Williams has learned the value of featuring periods of interactivity during some of his sermons. During one service in late 1999, Williams—who sits on a stool perched on a small platform at the front of the room—invited Mark Robinson, a recent convert, to join him up front for a question-and-answer period about the reliability of the Bible.

Williams began by introducing Robinson and asking him to tell a bit of his story. "I come from a dysfunctional family, like most people," said Robinson, who fascinated nearly 150 listeners with his tale of how he had "started my journey down the spiritual path," and how that journey led through Buddhism, Taoism, and ultimately to Christ through the ministry of Vanguard.

Brought to church by his wife (Robinson agreed to come "to keep the peace,") he talked about the night he had a vision of himself on a scavenger hunt. "I was going about this whole process of being spiritual, but I wasn't on the right track."

Soon after, Robinson picked up a Bible, which he first approached as just another spiritual book. But in time he came to believe it and trust it. Robinson's candid comments served as a lively introduction to Williams's sermon and helped provide a much-needed period of interaction for the people listening in.

New Models of Evangelism

During the 1960s and '70s, groups like Campus Crusade for Christ and Evangelism Explosion developed systematic approaches to evangelism that were hailed—both by their developers and many who used the techniques—for revolutionizing the challenging task of sharing the gospel with nonbelievers. But during the last decade, emerging Christian leaders have been doing some thinking of their own. So far, their experiments have yielded at least two new approaches.

1. Evangelism as Socratic Dialogue
In his 1995 book *Evangelism That Works*, pollster George Barna concluded that many of the ways Christians have tried to share their faith with others were ineffective. But he did uncover one approach that seemed to connect with members of Generations X and Y.

"One of the most interesting revelations from our research has been how positively baby busters respond to evangelistic efforts that use the Socratic method," he wrote.

In ancient Athens, various philosophers and instructors taught groups of young disciples using an instructional method that relied on a give-and-take process of questions and answers, engaging students in logical discussion and leading them to sound conclusions. Instead of blabbering on and on about what he knew, Socrates would invite students to share what they thought about the topic at hand, peppering them with questions and probing their answers for logical inconsistencies.

"The key to the Socratic method," wrote Barna, "is for the teacher to have mastered the matter under consideration so that he or she may ask probing, directive questions that do not manipulate the student so much as to help clarify the truth conclusion sought by the student."

Anyone who has ever overheard a group of busters sitting at a coffee bar debating the nature of the cosmos can immediately tell that the participants thoroughly enjoy the process of analyzing and debating reality. Socratic evangelism, which connects with this innate desire, seems to be a much better approach for provoking people to consider Christianity than older, more confrontational approaches that assume the Christian has all the answers in a neatly wrapped package and the listeners are hell-bent sinners in need of salvation.

"Busters…appreciate instructional methods that do not require tacit acceptance and rote memorization of imposed principles and truths," wrote Barna. "They have little trust for people who claim to know the truth or how to gain it."[5]

2. Evangelism as a Process

In one of his talks about ministry in the postmodern era, theologian Leonard Sweet observed that evangelism was less a matter of good guys and bad guys than it was a matter of folks in the process of finding God.

"Postmodern evangelism is recognizing that God is already at work in people's lives before we arrived on the scene," said Sweet, "and that our role is helping people to see how God is present and active in their lives, calling them home.

"Postmodern evangelism is not 'I have Jesus, and you don't. How can I get you here so that I can give you my Jesus?' but 'you already know Jesus, even if you don't think you know Jesus. How can I help you see and know what you already know?'"

Ken Baugh, the pastor of Frontline, the Gen X ministry of McLean Bible Church, calls this "process evangelism." "The whole idea of process evangelism in a nutshell is allowing people to be on a journey," he said, "and allowing them to experience Christ in a way that doesn't have to force the 'destination' of salvation. That's not to say we are excluding the destination, but the whole thing looks a little different in a postmodern world."

Baugh, who spent more than a decade in ministry at Saddleback Community Church, believes process evangelism represents a major change from the traditional approach to presenting the Christian faith.

"For the last twenty years of the modern era, we've used evangelism as a propositional, truth-telling format where we prove, either though archaeological evidence or through historical background, the validity and the authority of the Scriptures. But one of the ways postmodernism seems to express itself is through the idea that there is no such thing as absolute truth.

"So here we have a culture that doesn't adhere to standards of absolute truth, but truth claims are the main mechanism that we have used as our basic presuppositions. It's a disconnect. So what process evangelism does is it helps people discover Christ in the context of a relationship instead of in the context of being told that they're going to hell without Jesus Christ. Of course that's true, but the question is how we convey that to a postmodern world."

In practice that means that a month of Sundays may go by without Baugh issuing a formal altar call. "Part of the philosophy at Frontline and at McLean Bible Church as a whole is that people are in process, and we don't try to 'close the deal' every week," he explained. "When we do give an altar call, it flows out of a whole evening, and it's not some little thing we tack on to the end of the service every week, which I think minimizes it and makes it trite."

As another concession to postmodern realities, Baugh said, the church has "even gotten away from using the word 'Christian,' because the term 'Christian' has become so slimy in our culture these days, and it's been associated with so many divisive things and scandals. We like the term 'follower of Christ' better.

"The approach we take in our services is more like: 'Some of you are followers of Christ and you've been so for a long time. And some of you have yet to decide to follow Christ. Tonight I want to give you that opportunity. If you're at the place in your life where this is really starting to make sense, and you're ready to make that commitment, I want to give you that opportunity. But some of you are just not ready yet, and we want you to know that we're okay with that. We're not trying to force you or coerce you or manipulate you in any way. We respect your journey. We hope you get to that point, but we respect the journey that you're on.'

"We try to create an environment where it's okay for people to have questions, and where it's okay for people to say, 'No, that doesn't make sense' or 'I don't agree with that' or whatever. And part of the process is modeling Christ for people. People need to see that in order for that to be real."

Baugh said his approach has been criticized by some older pastors who say he is going soft on the gospel, but having looked at biblical examples, like Jesus' conversation with the woman at the well, he has concluded that he's not a heretic.

"If we were on the *Titanic* and it was going down, I'd be going to people and asking them if they knew Jesus," Baugh stated. "But at Frontline we have come to the point where as leaders we are okay with a person being in process and allowing them to leave our facility without making a decision for Christ that night. We know that God was working with them before they came to Frontline, and we know that he will be working with them after they leave. We simply trust them into the hands of God."

Messages for the Masses

One of the enduring images of evangelism during the second half of the twentieth century is a picture of Billy Graham at a podium in the center of a huge arena, where he is surrounded by thousands of people, beckoning them to make their way to the front and accept Christ while the crusade choir sings "Just As I Am."

Many people question whether there is a place for crusade evangelism in the new world, but thirty-two-year-old evangelist Jason Burden believes there is.

"A Gen Xer myself, I believe God has supernaturally given me the call and gift to unlock the neXt Generation's heart," said Burden, who along with author Stephen Bransford has devised a mass evangelism approach geared to younger people.

Burden called the first event, held in the fall of 2000, "Pierced," and he had two reasons for doing so. One is a passage in the gospel of John: "They will look on the one they have pierced" (19:37). Another is the growing popularity of body piercing, a practice Burden sees as a symbol of his generation's spiritual hunger.

"Busters possess a keen awareness and innate understanding of pain in the world and within themselves because of everything from government corruption to world famine," observed Burden, who gave his life to Christ at age seven, rebelled in his early teens, and rededicated his life to Christ at age nineteen before traveling the world with the Celebrant Singers and conducting evangelistic rallies.

"Gen Xers will say they pierce their bodies for cheap looks or to mark a significant life experience, but the underlying root is often a mixture of angst and hurt. Many who are not visibly pierced are inwardly torn apart. Xers are untrusting and cynical but, most of all, deeply wounded."

The initial Pierced event featured rock music, video clips, live video interaction, band member interviews, live art, and a stage drama. The culmination of Burden's sermon was an enactment of Jesus' crucifixion scene.

"Modern crusade evangelism does not work well with this generation because its goal is to prove the gospel objectively before the audience has had a chance to experience and consider it for themselves," noted Burden. "Xers crave interaction and will not accept Christ just because they are told to—that only initiates a cynical, knee-jerk response."

Living the Life

Nobody is claiming that evangelizing or discipling busters will be easy. Some young leaders compare the early years of the twenty-first century—with its resurgent paganism—to the early years of the first-century church, in which Christians presented the gospel to a pagan world.

But theologian Lesslie Newbigin has said that such comparisons miss an important point. "Today's paganism, having been born out of the rejection of Christianity, is far more resistant to the gospel than pre-Christian paganism," he explained.[6]

Thinkers like Donald Posterski, author of *Reinventing Evangelism*, believe today's Christians will have to give as much attention to living out the life as earlier generations did to proclaiming it throughout the world.

> In today's world, reinventing evangelism means that we
> must go beyond words. Our society desperately needs seri-
> ous followers of Jesus who will engage the culture with a
> coherent gospel....
>
> We need to become Christian *meaning-makers.*
> Meaning-makers are people who make sense of life,
> people who make sense of God, people whose lives ring
> with clarity in the midst of contemporary ambiguity,
> people who have integrity, people who reside in today's
> world revealing with their living and their lips that Jesus'
> death is the source of vital life.[7]

Posterski also believes Christians need to abandon impersonal methods that have been used in the past in favor of ways of relating that allow for personal connections and conversations. "Impersonal witnessing is like getting a birthday card from your insurance agent," he contended.[8]

Others agree. Kevin Ford, author of *Jesus for a New Generation,* wrote, "Individual Christians need to become the medium for the message." Ford and others call this an "embodied apologetic."

And hypocrisy, which has been a problem in the church for ages, could be a fatal failing today. In the past, preachers could get by with various inconsistencies, such as teaching about prayer while living personal lives that were too hectic for silence and solitude; or preaching about relationships while having no solid, intimate relationships of their own; or proclaiming the inherent God-given dignity of human life while repeating put-downs of women or members of other races or socioeconomic groups. But among the many cynical and cautious Xers, such behaviors provide such a powerful anti-apologetic that the seen gospel might overpower the preached one.

Perhaps many young leaders are once again learning the famous words of Saint Francis: "Preach always, and if necessary, use words."

whatever and ever, amen

Passion, Passivity, and New Ways of Making a Difference

One of the perennial images people have of members of the buster and millennial generations is that they are arrogant, self-centered, emotionally fragile sluggards who either are unwilling or unable to make deep and lasting commitments.

As author Richard Peace put it, busters "can't make commitments because they've never had much experience with commitments working out. Whenever they've made commitments in the past—to family, school, employers, relationships—they've gotten burned and bruised."

Or as the late musician Curt Cobain put it, "Oh, well, whatever, never mind."

But there are at least two sides to every story, and the nearly two thousand young people who spent part of a week in July 1998 fasting, praying, worshiping, weeping, and seeking God's will for their lives don't fit the slacker image. Summer events for Christian kids often challenge them to make commitments. But at this conference, hundreds of young people were volunteering to turn a blind eye to the ever-present temptations of the flesh, or even saying yes to service in a foreign country where Christians are routinely persecuted or killed.

"The main thing I preach about is challenging teens to live a life of radical holiness," said evangelist David Perkins, the then-twenty-one-year-old preacher who actually looks younger than his age and could pass for a member of rock music's sibling supergroup Hanson.

Perkins is convinced that people his age will respond to a challenging message of deep devotion if they hear it proclaimed and see it lived out by godly examples. "Kids respond to what they see," he said. "If they see a life of holiness and not just theory or preaching, they will grab on to that."

Nicole Sacks, age seventeen, agrees. The kids she knows desperately want to believe in and commit themselves to something. "Young people are either going to be Satanists or vampires or New Agers or Christians," said the Phoenix teenager. "If they could only see that God was more powerful than everything else, they would go with that."

Perkins and Sacks were just two of the people participating in Prayer Storm, a gathering that attracted young people from around the United States and several foreign countries. The event was sponsored by Rock the Nations, a ministry that, prior to shutting its doors early in 2000, organized big national events, smaller regional rallies, and in-school presentations.

Behind the scenes of its public activities, the ministry also ran a demanding Extreme Disciples Program that taught biblical basics to young people and encouraged them to give their lives in the service of God. One of the organization's rallying cries was "Mind-set of Martyrdom." In our post-Columbine era, when young people are increasingly aware that some of their fellow believers have been killed while proclaiming a belief in God, it wasn't a motto to be taken lightly.

Justin Burns and Josh Koenig, both nineteen years old, were part of the Extreme Disciples Program, a spiritual boot camp that involved young people in prayer, spiritual discipline, and ministry-related work.

"We want to have not just the title of Christian but the lifestyle of a Christian," said Burns. "The ED [Extreme Disciples] program has given me time to get my heart extremely fixed on God, to hear what the Lord is saying to me, and to get released from there to go to the mission field."

Koenig said the program's demands are tough. "They discipline hard, and they love hard. When they see areas of my life God wants to deal with, they walk me through those."

Gary Black, former president of Rock the Nations, said the organization's tough-love approach was the only way to reach a group he called "a fatherless generation." As many as one-third of today's young people don't live with their birth fathers, he observed, and untold numbers are living without the support and nurture of a spiritual mentor.

Many young people don't know how to begin to articulate the pain they have experienced in their lives. That's why Prayer Storm's intense periods of worship were so important.

"A lot of these kids live lives that are too painful to express," said Seth Peterson, a Prayer Storm worship leader. "But the Holy Spirit uses what they are singing. Many of them start to cry, but they don't even know why. And God starts the healing process there.

"Everything around young people today causes them to harden their hearts," Peterson added. "But worship softens their hearts. When they experience the presence of God, it disarms them."

Myths and Realities

Twenty-year-old Cassidy Dale gives presentations to older generations about the myths and realities surrounding Generation X.

Myth number one: Xers are disloyal and uncommitted. "They are not disloyal and uncommitted, as so many people claim, but rather they are cautious investors in a world which has taught them to expect little from institutional relationships," she clarified.

Another myth: Xers are selfish and arrogant. "The intense attitude expressed by so many Xers is not arrogance but rather a powerful independence which grows out of a life experience in which they have always felt they had only themselves to depend on at a very dangerous and unstable time in history."

It is true that members of the emerging generations are less likely than older Americans to participate in such rites of civic life as voting. A 1996 Yankelovich report comparing and contrasting busters, boomers, and the older "GI-generation" concluded that busters were skeptical about many politicians and much of the political process. Some analysts have even called them a "watcher generation," fearing that they will forever remain on the sidelines of the democratic process.

That fear is not as unreasonable as it might sound. Dante Chinni, an Xer who writes for *Newsweek*, explained some of this cynicism in a June 1997 article for the *Washington Monthly* magazine:

> Born in the late 1960s and 1970s, our experience has been
> a lengthy national losing streak. Ask anyone of my genera-
> tion what our era's defining moments have been and you
> will get different answers—Vietnam's conclusion, Nixon's

resignation, the Iran hostage crisis, the space shuttle explosion—but the answers will almost always be negative.…

Older people, who have lived through both the trials of the Depression and World War II, and the better times that followed, perceive the setbacks of the last twenty-five years as unfortunate moments on a long historical timeline. Our generation sees them as the timeline itself.[1]

Different Ways of Making a Difference

Even though many members of the emerging generations may be less politically active than earlier generations, that doesn't mean they've given up on having an impact on the world. Many younger people are substituting "personal activism"—serving in soup kitchens, cleaning up trash in parks, working with AIDS patients—instead of becoming involved in activities of a more political nature. Sanford Horwitt, a researcher who conducted a national study of the political attitudes of teenagers and young adults, reported that more than 90 percent of his subjects said that they believed helping others was the most important thing they could do as citizens.[2]

Boomers grew up in a culture that valued mass movements for causes like social justice, equal rights, and the end to the Vietnam War. Symbols of their ambitious activism could be found in big, celebrity-heavy events such as 1985's USA for Africa, which brought dozens of singers together to record the song "We Are the World," or in other events like Band Aid or Hands Across America. Boomers may have wanted to change the world, but in the eyes of many busters, they left it in shambles.

Some observers have concluded that busters, unlike boomers, are more realistic. They don't set out to change the world, but to make a difference. Or as Janet Bernardi expressed it in *A Generation Alone:* "Xers want to change the world, but they won't do it by standing on podiums and shaking their fists. They won't do it by linking arms and chanting slogans. They won't do it by shouting or dropping out or running for president. We Xers will change the world in a whisper—by changing the way we relate to one another as men and women, and as friends."[3]

The differing ways boomers and busters choose to live out their values and views illustrate the outlines of a significant generation gap. The jury is still out on whether America, as some older people suggest, is on the brink of a civic dark age in which widespread nonparticipation in politics will make the country vulnerable to undue influence or even a takeover by activists with minority viewpoints. Many younger people believe that's just about what has happened already.

But one thing is clear: People shouldn't mistake a lack of political involvement for a lack of concern or even action. In fact, there is evidence on many fronts that the emerging generations are more committed to social progress and more personally active in making a difference in the world than earlier generations.

A Flowering of Activism

When the Pacific Lumber Company threatened to cut down some of northern California's majestic redwood forests, twenty-three-year-old Julia Butterfly Hill went into action, scaling one of her beloved trees. She climbed the redwood in December 1997 and didn't come down until more than two years later, when she signed an agreement with the company that protected some of the forest.

In December 1999 economic leaders from some of the world's major countries came to Seattle for a meeting of the World Trade Organization. They encountered thousands of mostly Gen X protesters in a huge demonstration in the center of the city.

Such cases prove that activism isn't dead. Journalist Holly Lebowitz wrote about a resurgence of campus activism in the September-October 1999 issue of *Sojourners* magazine. "Contrary to the generally held view that today's college students are isolated, individualistic and concerned only with their Internet passwords and résumés," she wrote, "social justice activism is thriving on campuses around the country."[4]

Lebowitz cited numerous examples of how young people are involved in activism that reflects their values and beliefs:

- Students combining their concerns for environmentalism and social justice have created environmental groups at campuses across the country, including at the politically conservative Oral Roberts University.
- Many have enlisted in letter-writing campaigns, fasts, and other activities to address the horrible impact of homelessness, hunger, and poverty.
- Students at the University of Michigan organized a sit-in at the school president's Ann Arbor office to protest the exploitation of sweatshop laborers who produced official school clothing.
- Concerns about racial inequalities have led to the formation of numerous groups committed to promoting racial reconciliation and/or affirmative action programs.

- Worldwide religious persecution has motivated thousands of students to become involved in congressional lobbying campaigns and other activities.

Lebowitz observed that many religious leaders believe student activism is not only inspired by young people's faith commitments but also helps deepen those commitments. Meanwhile, many educators are so convinced that student activism is crucial to the future lives of the students and the country that they are building service requirements into the curriculum.

Just one sign of what some students want to do after graduation can be found in the fact that more graduates are becoming schoolteachers. "Interest in teaching...is being fueled by students' search for meaningful work, concern about the plight of at-risk children and a response to the national call for higher standards," wrote *New York Times* reporter Mary B. Tabor.

Young women who once rejected a future in teaching because it was perceived as a stereotypical female role have come to see that teaching is a powerful and rewarding way to shape young lives. And some young men are heading for careers in teaching after finding the corporate world dull and uninspiring.

"I just got a feeling for the corporate life and realized it wasn't for me," said one student, who was completing his work at a teaching college before heading off to a public school classroom.

What Can We Give?

During the 1990s some of the biggest boomer megachurches started adding health clubs, food courts, and other features to their facilities because their members wanted to take advantage of such services. But at some of the largest buster churches, the emphasis is on giving rather than getting.

At The Next Level Church in Denver, hundreds of young members volunteer at ministries and charities throughout the area. At Frontline in McLean, Virginia, members are involved in everything from offering free car washes to area residents, handing out free soft drinks at sporting events, putting money in parking meters, volunteering at area soup kitchens, or taking nearly sixty thousand dollars' worth of turkey dinners to nearly twenty-five thousand families throughout the Washington, D.C., area.

"We really emphasize sharing God's love in practical ways," said pastor Ken Baugh, who was inspired to emphasize practical service by the book *Getting Real* by Steve Schogrin, pastor of a Vineyard church in Cincinnati, Ohio.

"We need a place to demonstrate the validity of our faith and not just talk about our faith," noted Baugh. "We go and live out our faith in practical ways, demonstrating that there is something real here, not just lip service." He believes that the projects the church supports help the local community, but they also benefit the church. For one thing, people in the area have become aware that Frontline is a caring congregation.

"Our Thanksgiving project always gets a lot of media coverage, and you can't buy that kind of positive publicity," said Baugh. "But people who come in contact with us through our community work want to know more about us. One of the local TV reporters covering our Thanksgiving turkey outreach told me, 'I'm going to come back, and I'm bringing my family.'"

In addition, the various projects give the church a spiritual depth and an interpersonal intimacy that it wouldn't have if people merely came to services, sat there, and went home.

"It enables the average person to share their faith, where in normal circumstances they would be very intimidated to do so," said Baugh.

Frontline also encourages its members to participate in short-term missions trips. The church organized eleven such trips in 2000. "This is a great way to build community," Baugh observed.

Learning to Give It Away

Busters' hands-on approach to local service projects is changing the way many churches relate to their communities. In similar ways, their hands-on approach to charitable giving is transforming the philanthropic landscape.

The 1990s brought unprecedented wealth to many young people, with many techies making windfall profits from either working at one of the many new Internet companies or through investing in high-tech stocks. An article in *U.S. News & World Report* described how many of these young millionaires are giving money to their alma maters "in quantities never seen before."[5] Likewise, many are giving more to their churches or to various needy causes in their area.

Krue Brock is a thirty-one-year-old Georgia businessman who, along with his close friends, could serve as the poster boy for transforming the world of philanthropic giving. Like most Gen Xers, Brock places a premium on friendships and community, and these core values play an important role in how he gives.

About five years ago, he and nearly a dozen of the folks he went to high school with in Chattanooga formed a "giving circle," a small, informal, and flexible means for group members to share their lives with each other and their wealth with people who need it.

"I feel like I've been given about twelve friendships I need to be focused on in my life," said Brock. "I feel a responsibility to grow old with these people.

"We were all trying to figure out ways to stimulate and stir the relationships on a day-to-day basis, and we thought it would be a great idea to put some of our money together into a common pool and set some criteria for the way we would give it. We thought this would be a good way to be a part of something together and to have some accountability for our giving."

The twelve couples in the giving circle represent a wide range of occupations: three individuals are businessmen, but the group also includes a doctor, a veterinarian, a teacher, a college professor, an artist, a filmmaker, and two pastors. The circle members don't all have the same income levels, but that doesn't matter. Every couple is required to chip in at least 1 percent of their annual income, and most contribute much more.

Disbursements from the fund are handled in a relaxed and low-key manner. If three of the couples agree that a project should be funded, the circle gives whatever is needed, up to one thousand dollars. For grants of more than one thousand dollars, five couples must support the grant.

"The focus of giving areas is wide open, as long our people believe in it," Brock stated, and the group's 1999 giving proves his point. The circle, which was established under the auspices of the Chattanooga Community Foundation, gave money to an American seminary student, provided aid to survivors of hurricanes in Honduras, funded a ropes course at a local camp, bought a computer for a friend living in Kazakhstan, made a payment to another friend who works with single moms in St. Louis, sent kids on spring-break trips to Appalachia, underwrote programs for student leadership, sent a check to a small school in California, funded short-term mission trips for Christian young people, made grants to people ministering in inner cities and on college campuses, and made donations to Habitat for Humanity, Teen Challenge, and Chattanooga's Urban Art Institute.

While earlier generations of givers seemed largely content to do most of their giving at arm's length, writing checks to large organizations that were trusted to carry out the donors' wishes, today's givers place a premium on supporting work with which they have a sense of personal involvement and connectedness.

"One of the criteria we use is that we have to have some relationship with the work we are supporting," Brock remarked. "It's not just a cause-at-large. We want to give to something that fits with us. We don't just throw money out there. We try to be a part of what they are doing. It's easy to throw money out there, but it's hard to really be a part of people's lives."

And in their giving, the circle members care more about impact and immediacy than they do plaudits or write-offs.

"We don't want to restrict our giving to 501(c)3s," said Brock. "If there is a widow in the neighborhood who needs a sewer line put in, we are going to do that whether its through a 501(c)3 or not. A lot of people tell us that we shouldn't do that because it's not tax-deductible, but we're not trying to create tax deductions as much we are trying to be good givers."

Even though this approach worries some executives at traditional charities and parachurch organizations, the clear commitment to helping others indicates that Gen X isn't as selfish as some have suggested. The Chattanooga giving circle is just one of hundreds of such groups springing up in neighborhoods, at workplaces, and on college campuses throughout the country. These groups demonstrate that philanthropy, which has deep roots in America's faith-based communities, is alive and well.

Krue Brock and others like him present an inspiring example of the ways compassion can be linked with giving and personal involvement. Churches seeking to minister to younger believers must now ask themselves a new question: "Can we give these young people a big enough challenge to get them turned on and committed?"

where do we want to go today?

Swimming in a Sea of Pop Culture and Technology

Dogma, a film that makes lofty observations about faith while simultaneously winking at silly jokes about flatulence, is one of the most unusual religious movies ever made. Written and directed by Gen X filmmaker Kevin Smith, a self-confessed Catholic whose youthful imagination was steeped in comic books and videos, the 1999 movie illustrates the huge gulf separating the culture-embracing members of Generations X and Y from their often vehemently anti-pop-culture predecessors.

The film stars Matt Damon as Loki and Ben Affleck as Bartleby, two fallen angels with bad attitudes who were banished by God to the wasteland of Wisconsin. Now they'll do anything to get back home to heaven, even if it means they must exploit Roman Catholic canon law and even if their machinations threaten the sovereignty of God and the very existence of the cosmos.

God dispatches the glitzy angel Metatron (Alan Rickman) to earth, where he recruits a woman named Bethany (Linda Fiorentino) to join the battle against the renegade angels. A distant relative of Jesus, Bethany works in a Pittsburgh abortion clinic and is a mixture of faith and doubt. She reluctantly agrees to serve God and join the battle against evil.

Along the way, Bethany and Metatron encounter a muse (Salma Hayek) who works in a strip bar to make ends meet; Rufus (comedian Chris Rock), a previously unknown thirteenth disciple of Jesus who was allegedly edited out of the Bible because he was black; two unlikely prophets (Kevin Smith and Jason Mewes reprising their recurring roles as Silent Bob and Jay); and God (played by singer Alanis Morissette).

Other colorful characters include Cardinal Glick (George Carlin), whose program to reinvigorate the church is called "Catholicism—WOW!" and uses contemporary advertising and marketing techniques to replace the depressing image of the crucifix with a statue called "Buddy Christ," which features a smiling Jesus with upraised thumbs.

Smith, a film-school dropout and former video-store clerk, used credit cards to cover the costs of making his 1994 debut, *Clerks,* an acclaimed "slacker opus." In that film's closing credits, Smith thanks God, "without whom this couldn't have been done." His later explorations of baby buster ennui included 1995's *Mallrats* and 1997's *Chasing Amy.*

Raised in a strict, churchgoing Catholic home, Smith underwent a personal crisis of faith in his early twenties, which he once explained to the *New York Times:* "Sooner or later, no matter how devout you are, even if you're the Pope, you have to step back and say, 'What's the difference between this book, the Bible, and Greek mythology?'"[1]

A Film of Faith?

Dogma explores Smith's strong but often ambivalent feelings about religion. Although he has repeatedly affirmed his belief in God and in Jesus Christ, he is much less certain about the church. Like Bethany, a central character in *Dogma,* he goes to church but isn't always sure why and is usually bored. "It's called the celebration of the Mass, but it's no party," he said in an Internet interview. "No one's having a good time."[2]

Smith described *Dogma* as a comedic love letter to the church and the sacred mysteries of life, reminding viewers at the outset of the film that "God has a sense of humor." But many Catholic and Protestant groups weren't laughing. Some—including the Catholic League for Religious and Civil Rights, Donald Wildmon's American Family Association, and the Southern Baptist Convention—declared the film blasphemous, a charge that was disputed by Catholic priest and author Andrew Greeley.

"Is God offended by the movie?" Greeley asked in a column he wrote for Religion News Service. "Unlike those religious fanatics who are trying to ban the film, I claim no special access to the mind of the deity. I suspect, however, that God understands that the humor of the film is a prelude to making some very serious, and funny, theological points."

Still, the movie generated more prerelease opposition from religious conservatives than any film since 1988's *The Last Temptation of Christ,* a movie its director, Martin Scorsese, described as a "deeply religious film" but which Campus Crusade for Christ President Bill Bright offered to buy for $10 million so he could destroy it.

In both cases, religious leaders read early copies of the scripts, declared the movies blasphemous assaults on religious faith, and attempted to halt their release, unintentionally creating plentiful publicity for films that may have otherwise had little broad-based appeal.

Xers Embrace Pop Culture

Unlike certain church-related and parachurch groups, few members of the emerging generations boycotted *Dogma*. Many went to see it more than once. And some even viewed the film's release as an opportunity to explore contemporary perceptions of Christianity, viewing it with members of their congregations or with unchurched friends, with whom they discussed the movie for hours afterward.

Patton Dodd, a staff writer for New Life Church in Colorado Springs, Colorado, used the opening of *Dogma* as a chance to launch something he calls the Colorado Springs Film Society.

"My wife and I and a friend of ours were frustrated with knowing only Christians in Colorado Springs," Dodd explained. "All three of us work for ministries and have a difficult time meeting nonbelievers. We wanted to find a way to get involved in our community and get to know people outside our normal circle of influence. We are all interested in film, and we thought it'd be interesting and fun to develop a forum for the discussion of current movies.

"Soon, the local paper heard about us and ran a profile on the society. In time, more than three dozen people were coming to our meetings, where we would watch a film together and discuss it afterward. No one at the group knows we are Christians, and we don't plan on doing anything to show that we are other than forming relationships with people and letting the gospel speak through our lives."

Responses such as this show that, unlike older generations of Christians, younger believers don't view pop culture as part of a vast anti-Christian conspiracy. It's not that emerging generations don't see pop culture as a powerful forum for the expression of a wide variety of values and worldviews. To the contrary, they are much more astute at decoding pop culture and reading its metaphysical messages than most older Christians ever were. The difference is that they prefer to see pop culture as both a barometer and influencer of mainstream tastes and beliefs. Instead of seeking to silence or suppress it, they seek to understand it and utilize it in their ministries.

Throughout the 1990s, spiritual themes increasingly found their way into books, musical recordings, and films. Often these pop-culture artifacts raised deep and probing questions about the practice of Christianity (such as Robert Duvall's *The Apostle*) or gave glowing portrayals of non-Christian faiths such as Tibetan Buddhism (*Kundun* and *Seven Years in Tibet*). But instead of seeking to boycott or ban everything that they disagreed with, members of the emerging generations increasingly sought dialogue with the creators and consumers of the pop-culture cornucopia.

Christian pop-culture warriors spent much of the 1990s engaged in a battle with Disney. In the case of *Dogma*, they were successful in having a Disney subsidiary drop the film, but it was later picked up and distributed by another company. As Gen X authors Todd Hahn and David Verhaagen point out in their book *GenXers After God*, such battles only serve to illustrate the bankruptcy of the culture war approach. "On the surface we appear to be concerned with promoting godliness," they wrote.

However, a sharper analysis suggests that these skirmishes are more often motivated by fear. We are fearful that as Christians we are losing our place at the head of the table as the dominant molders and shapers of culture's mindset....

In our culture, we were comfortable with being the leaders of the consensus worldview. This is no longer true and it frightens us. In response we have lashed out.... The problem is that we have savaged the very ones that need the gospel. We have demonized them and turned them into our enemies.[3]

Hahn and Verhaagen describe a more redemptive approach in their book *Restless Hope:* "A better way is to honor and redeem the culture."

The Religious Right: R.I.P.

One of the most important evangelical books of 1999 was *Blinded by Might,* a heartfelt critique of the religious right written by two of its former lieutenants. Authors Ed Dobson and Cal Thomas both are former employees of Jerry Falwell's Moral Majority.

Founded in 1979, the Moral Majority quickly rose to national prominence, leading some of its leaders to believe that it had succeeded in reestablishing a lost sense of righteousness in American political life. "Had we not been Baptists, we would have danced in the streets," wrote Dobson of those heady, early days.

By the late 1990s, however, the religious right had suffered a series of embarrassing setbacks. "We failed," said Thomas, who is a columnist for the *Los Angeles Times* syndicate. "Very little that we set out to do has gotten done. In fact, the moral landscape of America has become worse."

Although the religious right helped change the direction of the national debate about morality and inspired a wave of political activism among previously apolitical believers, Dobson and Thomas take the position that the movement's sins far outweigh its virtues. These sins include pride (claiming that God was on their side alone), anger (demonizing ideological opponents), greed (raising money by exploiting people's fears about homosexuality), and lust (hungering for liberals' political power).

Dobson, a pastor's son who grew up in Northern Ireland, said that no matter where one lives, trying to make God and government the same thing brings unintended consequences. "When ministers merge religious passion with political zealotry, the net result is hatred," he observed.

New Ways of Engagement

Many busters have abandoned politics altogether, but not Christen Yates, who says believers should play a role in civic society. Still, Yates feels little sympathy for the bare-knuckle tactics and divisive "Christian America" rhetoric employed by many older Christian activists.

One of many young Christians working in and around the nation's capitol, Yates is the assistant program director for CIVITAS, an outreach of the Center for Public Justice (www.cpjustice.org) in Annapolis, Maryland.

She believes divisive rhetoric and combative approaches have helped to turn Capitol Hill into a modern-day Tower of Babel.

"We continue to feel the effects of this in the muddled babble among politicians, policy-makers, and philosophers," Yates noted. "We have made names for ourselves, but too often, these names are hostile and we speak them behind people's backs. Sadly, efforts to serve the Lord, to advance justice, and to transform public life become paralyzed when our focus shifts to ourselves and our talk becomes jargon."

Yates believes that America's continued survival and its hopes for "justice for all" depend on a "confessional pluralism" that allows multiple belief systems to thrive in a structurally pluralistic society. "As citizens, we are called to respect all belief systems equally," she said. "However, as Christians, we often do not apply this respect to each other."

Instead of love, Christians who disagree on the specifics of public policy battle one another. Unfortunately, Yates observed, harsh words lead to harsh actions and division.

"Ultimately, these contentions can trump the real power that evangelical Protestants and Catholics have in effecting change by factioning the body and deafening the voice," she remarked. "Have we forgotten Paul's chiding to the Corinthians, 'If I…can fathom all mysteries and all knowledge,… but have not love, I am nothing'?"

Many members of the emerging generations of Christians have almost totally forsaken the public square to focus on ministry within the church context. Others, like Yates, are seeking to continue the fight for biblically based public policies—a fight that was initiated by earlier generations. But she and others demonstrate a commitment to work for Christian values in the public square in more redemptive ways.

According to Tim Celek and Dieter Zander, authors of the 1996 book *Inside the Soul of a New Generation,* members of Generation X often view Christianity as an unnecessarily divisive faith, and they "view the church as being separatist, segregated, institutional, irrelevant, judgmental, holier-than-thou, controlling, authoritarian. And to some degree, they're right."

As for issues like abortion, homosexuality, and homosexual rights, which were hot-button issues for activists of the 1980s and 1990s, young people are much more accepting of the fact that a pluralistic society will have many people and lifestyles that differ from theirs. Though many worry about continued onslaughts on Christian morality, they don't think politics is the best or only way to promote righteous living.

Give Me That On-line Religion

Engineers at the University of Pennsylvania made history in 1946 when they assembled eighteen thousand vacuum tubes and miles of wire into a thirty-ton monstrosity called the Electronic Numerical Integrator and Calculator, or ENIAC, the world's first multipurpose electronic computer. But by 1971 all of ENIAC's computing power could be squeezed onto a tiny silicon wafer the size of a postage stamp. And a few years later, the home computer revolution was under way.

Just as baby boomers grew up in the soft glow of television screens, those who came after them grew up computing. Department of Defense engineers first linked computers at four American university campuses in 1969. And in 1991, Tim Berners-Lee published his first programming code for the World Wide Web, which rapidly transformed the way people shopped, studied, and invested. By the mid-1990s, millions of individuals were cruising the information superhighway, where they could find everything from on-line prayer groups to sites about pedophilia and bestiality.

The untamed openness of the Internet worried many conservative evangelicals, some of whom unsuccessfully sought to control its content or limit access to its seedier sites. Others boldly ventured into cyberspace to promote the gospel. As Jason Baker wrote in *Christian Cyberspace Companion:* "Throughout church history, Christians have witnessed numerous technological advancements. Some of these, such as movable type, have been well harnessed to produce great benefits for the church. In the last decade, the explosion of personal computers brought irrevocable changes to the way people work and play. Fortunately, pioneering Christians sought ways to employ this technology on the personal and corporate levels."[4]

Walt Wilson, author of *The Internet Church,* agrees, arguing that the rapid worldwide growth of the Web is part of a divine plan.

"It is not about technology; it is about the Great Commission," Wilson told Leadership Network's *Explorer* e-newsletter. "This is not about man's inventions or his creative schemes. These developments are about something much bigger and far more dramatic. In fact, these events are not about technology at all. Change this big is being orchestrated by God, not by us."

Wilson is not alone in believing that the Internet age presents a new opportunity for the church. "We tend to think of the church in terms of being very local and geographic in nature," he wrote. "But in terms of outreach and ministry, we are now thrust into a borderless, timeless world."[5]

An interview posted on theWeb site operated by the Ooze, a network of Gen X ministries, was even more enthusiastic. In "The 640x480 Window:

Leveraging the Web for Ministry in a Digital World," Internet executive John Carley said, "As the Internet expands at a screaming pace, many churches and ministries are catching on to the idea that the web is the next great missionary field. In addition to the 10/40 window, some churches are beginning to take notice of the 640x480 windows," a reference to the multi-hued pixels of a computer screen.[6]

By the late 1990s, churches, ministries, organizations, and companies were flocking to cyberspace, where they were setting up hundreds of Web sites to promote their work or sell books, Bibles, music, and videos.

But not all Christians were gung ho about virtual religion. In his thoughtful book *The Soul in Cyberspace,* Douglas Groothuis sounded a warning about the implicit gnosticism of the Internet and "the danger of the technological replacement of the personal." He wrote: "An artificial and impersonal means of communication replaces human interaction in ways that are not immediately obvious. In so doing, it debases the personal dimension God values so highly."

As with other forms of culture, it wasn't just Christians promoting their wares. The Internet gave millions of people access to a spiritual cornucopia, as many alternative religious movements set up sites in cyberspace. According to Jeff Zaleski, a former editor of *Parabola* magazine and author of *The Soul of Cyberspace,* on the Internet all faiths are equal. "How will this ease of access to the universal store of sacred knowledge reshape the spiritual life of our species? Will religions keep their belief systems and their body of believers intact in a virtual world where it takes only a click of a mouse to jump from one temple, one mosque, one church to the next? Questions like these promised to keep Christians occupied well into the 21st century."[7]

For young Christians, the religious diversity of cyberspace is little more than a reflection of the pluralism they have grown up in. While a few of them may view the Web as some kind of electronic utopia, most are more grounded, seeing it as a powerful tool but not a panacea.

Pop-Culture Spirituality

During the twentieth century, Christians exhibited one of two contradictory approaches toward popular culture, according to author and Calvin College professor Bill Romanowski. On the one hand, they condemned it as "trivial, mindless, and escapist amusement." On the other hand, they charged it with the "debasement of taste and the destruction of values" in our society. But as he argued in his 1996 book *Pop Culture Wars,* "entertainment cannot be trivial and dangerous at the same time; it is either one or the other."

In the 1980s and 1990s, pop culture was being condemned by many, but at the same time there was growing agreement that all forms of pop culture were becoming increasingly powerful vehicles for spiritual views of all kinds. And as more and more people became spiritual "seekers," many of them did some of their best seeking in stores carrying a growing array of spiritual products.

Take bookstores, for example. During the last half of the 1990s, the rage in Christian bookstores was the multi-million-selling Left Behind series of end-times novels coauthored by Tim LaHaye and Jerry Jenkins. The series spawned a mini-industry of related products and a Web site (www.leftbehind.com) and reportedly inspired thousands of readers to prepare for meeting their Maker.

The Left Behind books were selling in mainstream stores, too, alongside a growing variety of books from Buddhist, New Age, and other approaches. Surprisingly, books by Christian writers like Kathleen Norris and Anne Lamott became national bestsellers.

Norris had abandoned the Protestant pieties of her childhood for the life of a poet in New York City, but in the early 1980s, a hunger she describes as "a vague desire for more spiritual depth in my life" led her to reexamine Christian traditions. In the process, she found them "much more various, rich, and nourishing than I had ever imagined."

In *The Cloister Walk*, Norris introduced readers to the rhythms and mysteries of monasticism, which she had experienced firsthand during nine months as an oblate (or lay associate) at a Benedictine monastery. Her next book, 1998's *Amazing Grace: A Vocabulary of Faith*, offered readers lively, literary interpretations of concepts like salvation, incarnation, repentance, and orthodoxy, as well as dozens of other perplexing Protestant terms she encountered at Spencer Memorial Presbyterian Church in Lemmon, South Dakota.

"When I first ventured back to Sunday worship in my small town, the services felt like a word bombardment, an hour-long barrage of heavyweight theological terminology," she wrote. "Often, I was so exhausted afterwards that I would need a three-hour nap."

Her ability to communicate to such a broad spectrum of readers is just one of Norris's rare gifts, and it's one that has allowed her to ride the crest of the current wave of interest in spirituality. *The Cloister Walk* was on the *New York Times* hardback bestseller list for more than four months, was the subject of a story on the Jesuit-run Vatican radio, and was excerpted in both

New Age Journal and the evangelical *Christianity Today* (which also named it one of the year's best books).

"I think we're seeing the fruit of a lot of well-meaning people in the sixties who said we're going to raise the kids with no religion," said Norris in an interview. "As a result, people are frantically searching for some religious meaning in their lives. And they're sort of taking whatever shows up, which is a really unwise thing. If you raise people with no religion, they will wind up with some really warped religions."

Anne Lamott's *Traveling Mercies: Some Thoughts on Faith,* a 1999 *New York Times* bestseller, was a passionate and earthy memoir of the author's troubled pilgrimage to her Christian rebirth. Lamott's idiosyncratic views and rough language meant that most Christian bookstores wouldn't carry the book, but its success in mainstream stores indicated that many readers were interested in this literate and moving memoir of conversion and faith.

Music of the Spheres

As the last millennium was winding down, a number of popular recording artists were getting serious about the meaning of life, producing a bumper crop of best-selling albums that brimmed with spiritual and philosophical themes.

The Fragile, an angst-filled sonic wail of sometimes beautiful but nearly always nihilistic industrial rock by Nine Inch Nails, debuted atop *Billboard*'s national sales chart in October 1999 before being replaced by Creed's *Human Clay,* a collection of muscular hard rock that runneth over with religious themes. Then it was Latin rock legend Carlos Santana's *Supernatural* album—with its music that, according to the promotional copy, "touches each listener directly in the heart and stirs the soul"—that dominated the charts and the 2000 Grammy Awards.

"Even now, with nookie and cash ruling the scene, divine hunger still motivates some rockers," wrote a *Rolling Stone* reviewer, who added that spiritual songs "appeal to young people who grew up swabbed by catechism, Bible study, or Hebrew school." A *Spin* magazine writer commented on the metaphysical musings of artists like Madonna, Alanis Morissette, and Jewel, saying, "The dividing line between the spirit and the entertainment industry is becoming increasingly tough to draw."[8]

The albums by Nine Inch Nails and Creed offer intriguing perspectives on Gen X spirituality. Issues of meaning—and meaninglessness—are at the heart of Nine Inch Nails's *The Fragile*, an album the *New York Times* called "a desperate identity crisis rendered in symphonic scale."[9] *The Fragile* features Trent Reznor's bracing lyrics, his ragged vocals and screams, and a dazzling and obsessively crafted soundscape of acoustic instruments, electronic sounds, and synthesized noise. Alternately beautiful and horrifying, the album is a perfect accompaniment for the end of the world.

On the opposite side of pop music's philosophical divide is Creed, whose music affirms the existence of God and the possibility of human transformation. The band's debut album, *My Own Prison*, has sold nearly four million copies, and *Human Clay*, their hard-rocking sophomore outing, has already sold a million.

Creed's lead vocalist, Scott Stapp, is a preacher's kid who says he still hasn't found what he's looking for and rarely comments on his own beliefs. "When the secular media asks me questions, 90 percent of them have no background in religion, so they don't even understand," he said during one recent interview, adding, "I know that I believe in God."[10]

Mystical Movies

Four of the five "Best Picture" nominees for the 2000 Academy Awards were films that dealt with explicitly spiritual themes: *American Beauty, The Cider House Rules, The Sixth Sense,* and *The Green Mile.* But this came as no real surprise to members of the emerging generations. For them, movies like *Star Wars* had served as a sort of electronic nursery rhyme, and trips to the cineplex often had been more spiritually rewarding than Sunday mornings at church.

Busters grew up with *Star Wars* (1977), *The Empire Strikes Back* (1980), and *Return of the Jedi* (1983). Although their special effects now look hokey, the message of the films endures.

"I put the Force into the movie in order to try to awaken a certain kind of spirituality in young people—more a belief in God than a belief in any particular religious system," said Star Wars creator George Lucas in a *Time* magazine interview with Bill Moyers.[11] Lucas, who possesses a unique ability to blend entertainment and enlightenment, filled his Star Wars films with a mixture of matinee melodrama, science-fiction fantasy, Old West gunslinging, and samurai swordsmanship.

The films' theology is equally eclectic, serving up a syncretistic sampling of Christian themes (the battle between good and evil and ultimate redemption), ancient Eastern philosophy (the all-is-one pantheism of the Force), and New Agey human potentiality. ("Concentrate on the moment," Jedi master Qui-Gon Jinn tells young Anakin Skywalker. "Feel, don't think. Use your instincts.")

Lucas also employs timeless mythological motifs such as the hero, the dream, and the journey of transformation, all of which are aspects of something the late Joseph Campbell called the Western world's "monomyth." And both the good guys and the bad guys in the Star Wars films have a system of spiritual apprenticeship that resembles Eastern religions' tradition of masters, or gurus.

In *The Phantom Menace,* Jedi master Qui-Gon Jinn (Liam Neeson) instructs a young Obi-Wan Kenobi (Ewan McGregor) in the ways of the Force. "Nothing happens by accident," says Qui-Gon at one point.

In 1999 millions of fans lined up to get their tickets to *The Phantom Menace,* a film whose release "ranks right up there with the Second Coming of Christ," according to a *Newsweek* writer.[12] But the Institute for Creation Research, based in El Cajon, California, saw more sinister intentions at work in the film.

In "The Menace of the Force," a program the biblical creationism advocacy organization created for broadcast on Christian radio stations, the film series was portrayed as a celluloid Trojan horse, exposing unsuspecting moviegoers to anti-Christian theologies. "Satan has used very modern tools to ease his New Age lies into the mainstream," said a narrator in the program.

The Star Wars films weren't the only movies to reveal the vast cultural divide separating members of Generations X and Y from older believers. Busters and millennials of many religious persuasions were intrigued by *The Matrix,* a film that combined cyberpunk sensibilities with plentiful Christian metaphors. But older folks didn't get it, and many merely objected to the film's rampant and visually stunning sci-fi violence.

A Mass-Media Mecca

Although films like *The Matrix* paid homage to Christian concepts, there were other times when it seemed that other faiths ruled pop culture.

In 1998, Wicca, a contemporary, neo-pagan form of witchcraft, was enjoying unprecedented positive media coverage. *Practical Magic,* a light-hearted film, featured Sandra Bullock and Nicole Kidman as two modern-day witches who were trying to decide whether to use ancient spells and mystical arts in their search for happiness and love.

About the same time, New York City attorney and witch Phyllis Curott was crisscrossing America on a twenty-one-city publicity tour for her semi-autobiographical work *Book of Shadows.* And witchy TV shows like ABC's *Sabrina, the Teenage Witch* and the WB network's *Charmed* were getting good ratings. Wiccan concepts also were showing up in print ads for Cover Girl makeup and Finesse shampoo. At the same time, some universities and divinity programs were offering degrees in goddess spirituality, and the Internet was teeming with witchcraft-related sites, many of which helped connect on-line seekers with local covens. Wicca, as a *Fitness* magazine headline proclaimed, is "Coming Out of the Broom Closet."

Busters and millennials weren't particularly troubled by all the hubbub over Wicca, but should they have been? Were members of the emerging generations simply too accepting of pop culture's mixed messages? Were they oblivious to the implications of the spiritually charged sea in which they swam? Certainly many older believers thought so.

Also troubling to many elders was the easy availability of pornography. In the 1980s, James Dobson of Focus on the Family had worked with government leaders to fight against porn, and he even called his efforts "a winnable war." But by the late 1990s, it was clear that porn had won. According to a Nielsen NetRatings survey, 17.5 million Americans had Web surfed to porn sites in January 2000, and one site even boasted that it had more on-line visitors during the month than "legitimate" sites like ESPN.com and barnesandnoble.com.

Few buster thinkers condemned pop-culture content, but some did challenge young believers to fast from mass media consumption, much as earlier generations of believers had regularly fasted from food and drink. By practicing disciplined consumption, they said, members of Generations X and Y could avoid being poisoned by pop culture's more polluted waters.

part 3

reinventing the church

new day, new wineskins

Emerging Leaders Remaking the Church

Things were tense in May 1998 when young leaders of some of the nation's newest cutting-edge churches were invited to talk about "Understanding Ministry to Generation X'ers" at a Southern Baptist–sponsored Innovative Church Leadership Conference. The tensions at the event sprang from intense disagreements over two issues.

One was the spiritual health of the contemporary American church. Some young leaders strongly believed the boomer pastors of America's leading megachurches have given up biblically based ecclesiology for a culturally determined, marketing-oriented model, sacrificing spiritual depth for numerical growth.

A second concern was the future direction of the American church. Here the younger leaders disagreed among themselves about which ecclesiastical models were most valid. Some preferred stripped-down, house-church models that hearken back to the first-century believers. Others seemingly were content to tweak boomer models by simply adding music that is rawer and rougher than the boomers' praise choruses and by wearing clothing that is darker and less formal than Willow Creek Community Church's famous color-coordinated pastels.

One thing nearly everybody agreed on is that many young people may never attend their parents' churches, so young leaders are busily creating their own approaches to doing church that will enable them to reach their own largely unreached generations.

Theoretically, there are as many ways to do postmodern, generationally relevant ministry as there are people doing it. But over the last five years, most of the new efforts have fallen into one of the following five categories:

- *"Underground" efforts.* Many busters have decided to work outside the walls of existing churches and instead concentrate on incarnational ministry through music, art, coffee houses, or other non-ecclesiastical expressions.

- *Youth ministry and/or campus ministry.* Often operating as programs within larger churches, these specialized ministries usually deal with generational issues before the larger church does.

- *Targeted services or programs.* Many churches have launched Saturday or Sunday evening services designed for busters, or they offer other targeted programs at the church or off-site at some other time during the week. This approach allows churches to stick their toes in the water without diving all the way in; it also has all the advantages and disadvantages that come with such halfway efforts.

- A *church-within-a-church.* More than a program but less than an independent church, these efforts allow an evolving Gen X congregation to form, grow, and achieve a measure of community within the context of a supportive parent church. The experiences of this type that have worked the best are those like Frontline, the nation's largest church-within-a-church ministry, where there is deep trust among the elder and younger pastors.

- *Church plant of a new congregation.* Churches like Mars Hill and Pathways are new churches. This approach allows young leaders the greatest freedom to create their own philosophy, staff, and style of worship. However, it also saddles young leaders and congregations with all the responsibilities of running a church, and some efforts have not survived the strain.

In this chapter we will focus primarily on examples of the two most common models: church-within-a-church and church plant. But before doing so, let's take a brief look at the recent history of the church in America, paying special attention to some of the issues that cause the most grief for young leaders.

Selling Salvation

Many of the debates over America's churches begin with the way the Christian life is packaged and promoted to nonbelievers in evangelistic campaigns and methodology.

In 1967 three dozen pastors attended Evangelism Explosion's first leadership training clinic. EE, the brainchild of the Reverend D. James Kennedy of Coral Ridge Presbyterian Church in Fort Lauderdale, Florida, promoted Kennedy's vision of "mobilizing and equipping the vast lay army of the church to do the work of ministry."

In 1970 Kennedy's methods were published in the *Evangelism Explosion* textbook, which *Christianity Today* called "probably the most widely used single guide" for evangelism. By 1973 the program had gone international, and by 1995 it had fulfilled the ministry's goal of operating in all 211 of the world's nations.

Over the years, EE has helped thousands of Christians overcome their fears of presenting the gospel to others. At the same time, it and other evangelism programs have been criticized for marketing the Christian faith like any other consumer product, emphasizing its potential benefits and downplaying its true costs.

"There are five great laws of selling or persuading: attention, interest, desire, conviction, and close," wrote Kennedy in *Evangelism Explosion*. "It does not matter whether you are selling a refrigerator or persuading men to accept a new idea or philosophy, the same basic laws of persuasion hold true."

Likewise, Bill Bright, founder and president of Campus Crusade for Christ, boiled salvation down to the Four Spiritual Laws, which emphasized the benefits of individual salvation ("God has a wonderful plan for your life"). First published in tract form in 1965, there have since been more than one billion copies of the laws printed and distributed throughout the world.

In the mid-1970s, Bright took the selling of salvation to unprecedented heights with his Here's Life, America! campaign, which aimed at nothing less than the evangelization of America by 1977 and the world by 1980. A 1977 article in *Time* magazine summarized the campaign: "Here's Life markets Jesus the way others might introduce a new brand of soda pop to a city. I FOUND IT! tease the TV and newspaper ads, billboards, buttons, bumper stickers. Found what? The ads offer a telephone number that will provide the answer: Jesus."

By 1978 the campaign had reached more than one hundred countries and recorded more than 3.5 million decisions for Christ, but it also generated criticism. Billy Graham, whose evangelistic crusades depended on the participation of local churches, asked Bright to remove his name from the campaign's list of supporters, saying the parachurch powerhouse seemed to be "in competition with the churches." An article in the *Christian Century* criticized the campaign's gimmickry and exploitation of people's emotions as well as its faulty theology of both witness and salvation. "Christ's claim of Lordship over the whole of human history and the costly call to discipleship become lost in the presentation of 'new life' as a possession to be added to the other possessions of television viewers and telephone callers," the magazine stated. "The glorious gospel becomes a commodity sold and delivered to the doorstep like a brush or a bar of soap."

Hard-sell evangelism campaigns were critiqued in Joseph Bayly's *The Gospel Blimp*, which used metaphor and satire to deliver a stinging message: "Jesus Christ didn't commit the gospel to an advertising agency; He commissioned disciples. And He didn't command them to put up signs and pass out tracts; He said that they would be His witnesses."[1]

Marketing the Church

In the 1980s and 1990s, the marketing model that inspired the big evangelistic campaigns of the sixties and seventies was imported wholesale into many churches. That process culminated in a situation that, according to George Hunsberger of the Gospel and Our Culture Network, reduced churches to the role of being "basically a vendor of religious goods and services in a competitive religious marketplace."

George Barna's 1988 book *Marketing the Church* was the bible for the new movement. "My contention," Barna wrote, "based on careful study of data and the activities of American churches, is that the major problem plaguing the Church is its failure to embrace a marketing orientation in what has become a marketing-driven environment."[2]

Barna urged his readers to "suspend any attachments to traditional thinking about church growth," telling readers, "Think of your church not as a religious meeting place, but as a service agency—an entity that exists to satisfy people's needs."[3]

With the publication of *Marketing the Church,* Barna radically reinterpreted much of the New Testament in terms of religious free enterprise, calling the church "a business...involved in the business of ministry"; describing the Bible as "one of the world's great marketing texts"; hailing Jesus as a master "of the data gathering and analysis process"; claiming Paul's "entire public ministry was based on a continual environmental assessment"; and summarizing the disciples as "an informed, capable distribution system."

As for Jesus' parable of the sower and the seed, it "portrays marketing the faith as a process in which there are hot prospects and not-so-hot prospects and shows how we should gear our efforts toward the greatest productivity."[4]

Barna's marketing-oriented gospel attracted eager disciples. And no church applied these methods more aggressively or with as much numerical success as Willow Creek Community Church, a church of nearly seventeen thousand people located in a $34 million complex in South Barrington, Illinois.

Senior Pastor Bill Hybels, a former youth minister, used consumer research, niche marketing, and contemporary communications and management theory to build his church. Thanks to its Willow Creek Association, which has more than four thousand member churches; its popular training sessions, which have tutored more than fifty thousand pastors; and its numerous publishing projects, Willow Creek became the most influential and most frequently copied church during the last decade of the twentieth century.

Willow Creek places top priority on evangelizing nonbelievers through its carefully choreographed seeker-sensitive services, which are designed to entertain, relax, and ultimately persuade well-educated, upscale, white baby boomers.

As Hybels explained to a group of pastors, "What does the seeker walk into in ninety-nine out of one hundred churches across this land? He walks into a service that has been designed from stem to stern for the already convinced. It's a worship service."

Scholar Greg Pritchard, author of *Willow Creek Seeker Services,* a thoroughly researched book-length study of the church's methodology, claimed that 80 percent of the people attending Willow Creek's seeker services are Christians, not "seekers," and that relatively few people participate in discipleship and teaching small groups or make any meaningful connections with other attendees. Echoing the words of Bayly's *Gospel Blimp,* Pritchard concludes, "The Gospel is not a Big Mac, and Jesus did not die as the first step in a marketing plan."

Church historian Bruce Shelley and his son, Marshall Shelley, argue in their 1992 book *The Consumer Church* that the church's emphasis on marketing has baptized consumerism and compromised the gospel: "Unlike the rich young ruler in the Gospels, church attenders seldom ask, 'What must I do?' They are far more likely to ask, 'What do I get out of this?'"

McChurch?

Some busters agree with sociologist Dennis W. Hiebert, who argued in the Winter 1999 issue of *Christian Scholar's Review* that American Protestantism has been "McDonaldized," meaning that many churches have placed top priority on four main values: efficiency, calculability, predictability, and control.

People earnestly debate whether such values produce healthy churches. But Hiebert argued that "any good principle, taken to the extreme, becomes grotesque," and he suggested that some churches have gone overboard, to the point that God will be locked out and people will be denied transforming spiritual experiences.

The overmanaged, overengineered church, Hiebert confirmed, "will simply confirm the suspicion that the church is really not fundamentally different from other humanly constructed organizations."

McChurch ecclesiology bothers some theologians and scholars, but it deeply troubles many busters. In Douglas Coupland's *Generation X,* one of the chapters is entitled, "I Am Not a Target Market." And buster pastor Todd Hahn underscored the point: "To us, most churches are trying to sell something that many of us don't want. We want something authentic and genuine."

170

But Hahn, pastor of Charlotte's Warehouse 242, also wants it to be known that he believes the seeker-sensitive model has done much good for many churches. "Any model is going to have weak sides and strong sides," he observed. "The part we've been influenced by is the fact that the church ought to think intentionally in what it does about reaching people who are outside the faith.

"Of course, the flaw in the seeker model is that if your seeker service is the main gathering for your church, where do you do your discipleship for believers? That's a challenge, but it's not a fatal flaw. In my mind, the fatal flaw is in the traditional church that does nothing to reach nonbelievers.

"We are vehement in rejecting that, but what we are also recognizing is that there is a cultural shift from the modern era to the postmodern era, where even people outside the faith want to experience transcendent reality in some way. They're not afraid of spirituality. They're not even afraid of spiritual symbols."

Graceland: A Church Within a Church

Santa Cruz, located south of San Francisco, is a sun-drenched oceanside city of fifty thousand people. The Santa Cruz Bible Church is a solid and growing church patterned after the modern mold. But there was one problem: Many of the church's young people weren't making the transition from being active members of youth programs to regular attenders of the church.

In 1997, Dan Kimball, who led the church's high-school youth group for much of the 1990s, launched Graceland (www.santacruzbible.org/graceland), a Gen X–oriented church within the larger congregation. Although the two congregations meet in the same building and share the same creedal affirmations, they couldn't be more different. One visitor told Kimball that Graceland was as far away from the seeker-sensitive megachurch model as anything he had seen.

"In the summer of 1995, we started holding services where we unplugged the instruments and lit candles," Kimball told *Youthworker Journal.* "I was seeing something different—'harder' kids were participating. I thought we needed to use gizmos and gimmicks, but kids were responding to stripped-down, raw stuff."

The differences at Graceland start with the sacred environment Kimball tries to create before a single word is said or sung. The lights in the sanctuary are turned down, and the worship area is decorated with candles. Images of stained-glass windows are projected onto screens.

The service features a mixture of old and new worship songs and hymns, as well as corporate readings from the Bible or sometimes ancient church creeds.

Even though Kimball wasn't pursuing numerical growth at any cost, Graceland's two Sunday evening services now attract as many as eight hundred people a week, including high schoolers, college-age kids, married couples, and even some parents.

"It seems the more spiritual we get, the more response we get," Kimball observed. "All the comments I hear are that young people want more of the raw, spiritual, mystical aspects of the church."

Starting a new church within an existing older congregation is one of the more popular ways of reaching the emerging generations. And those who advocate this approach believe it has clear advantages over planting a new congregation.

For one, the new church can use the existing church's resources, including its building (which typically has to be decorated in different styles for its different services), as well as its support staff, including everyone from receptionists to custodians.

More important, churches within churches provide continuity between the generations instead of separating young and old into totally distinct operations. In Santa Cruz, members of Graceland and the parent Bible church come together at an annual all-church Memorial Day picnic. And for Easter 1999 both "churches" cooperated in organizing an all-church worship celebration that borrowed from both modern and postmodern approaches.

In addition, older members of the church help with vital leadership roles in Graceland, and many members of the parent church help mentor members of the younger body.

The most important thing that is required for this approach to succeed is the support of the church's senior pastor, and Kimball asserted he has that in full. Specifically, he said Santa Cruz senior pastor Chip Ingram saw that the main church wasn't doing an effective job of reaching young people. In addition, Ingram trusted Kimball enough to launch the new venture, and Ingram didn't feel threatened by a "competing" church meeting in his own building.

In a *Youthworker Journal* article, Ingram described it this way: "With Dan, I thought, 'Here's a guy who's 35 and gifted in reaching postmoderns. I know I'm not the person who's going to reach them. And we're going to lose them if we don't let Dan dream his dreams.' So Graceland was not a big leap."

Ingram, who preaches at Graceland services three times a year, added that "success is not focusing on how many people think you're the hot shot, it's equipping your leaders to help others grow. That's the calling. It's not about getting credit."

Kimball believes the approach he has taken allows for a specialized ministry while not destroying the precious unity of the body of Christ.

"It's a shame that when churches 'get older,' all the young people and younger families leave and go to the new, hot church in town. With the 'church within a church' model, that's not necessary."

Church Plant: Rock Harbor Church

Keith Page, the thirty-six-year-old pastor of Rock Harbor Church in Costa Mesa, California, has a strong partnership with his parent congregation, Mariners Church, an Orange County megachurch. But the two are separate entities, and that's the way they like it. The official parting was as well orchestrated as a megachurch worship service.

It started with a period of vision-casting that began years before the new church was born. Then one year before the launch of Rock Harbor, the congregation was brought in on the process. At a Mariners worship service, senior pastors announced that the congregation planned to start a new sister congregation, "God willing."

During the following year, staffing and supervision issues were resolved. Five couples from Mariners agreed to commit to help the new congregation for a period of one year. In addition, four members of the parent church agreed to serve on Rock Harbor's board for its first year.

When it was nearing time for the parting, the church hosted a Sunday evening dessert for 250 people where it outlined the vision of the new congregation. And the Sunday before Rock Harbor's first service, a love offering was taken to help with finances.

Speaking of finances, Mariners agreed to pay Page's salary during his first year as pastor of Rock Harbor. By month thirteen, that support dropped to 75 percent of his salary. Two months later, it dropped to 50 percent. Two months later Page received 25 percent of his salary from Mariners, and two months later he was totally self-supporting.

Members of Mariners helped give Rock Harbor a happy inaugural Sunday, when five hundred people turned out to attend a service at the Costa Mesa Senior Center, which served as the new church's first home. Interestingly, their presence at the center helped Rock Harbor reach beyond its own generational limitations, and Page said he even baptized one of the center's eighty-year-old regulars.

By mid-2000, Rock Harbor was enjoying regular attendance of eighteen hundred people, employed twenty full-time staffers, and had launched a one-million-dollar building campaign, all of which was making Page a bit nervous. As he told the *Los Angeles Times,* he hoped that all the growth and the new emphasis on a permanent facility wouldn't lead people to see the church as a building instead of as a body of believers.[5]

The two congregations still maintain many similarities, but Page said that his young church plant has a number of distinctives, including its more up-tempo worship music, its periods of stillness and silence, a greater emphasis on sermons that "speak to people where they're at," and a laid-back approach that is designed "for people wanting something that isn't as polished as a traditional boomer service."

Page admitted that he and other members of his generation have been turned off by church services that "run so smoothly they come across as fake," but now he wrestles with the challenge of maintaining Rock Harbor's creative edge. "We're trying to figure out how not to be 'polished' but to still be professional," he said.

Like Dan Kimball at Graceland, Page said he couldn't have started Rock Harbor without his own pastor's grace, humility, and insight.

"For many senior pastors, their biggest hurdle is getting over their own fear," noted Page. "Many pastors are petrified about giving away any areas of key leadership. And understandably, they are concerned about losing members to a new congregation.

"For some pastors, the question they have is, 'Can we still live our dream as a church with a significant leakage of people?' Another question is whether a senior pastor can smile and say, 'God bless you. Go.'"

Saying "go" is always difficult, but in many cases it doesn't mean saying good-bye. Rock Harbor and Mariners still maintain strong bonds, and the pastors of each congregation publicly support each other, even if they now do so from different facilities.

A Church in Transition

Warehouse 242 got its start in 1996 as a targeted subministry of Forest Hill Presbyterian Church in Charlotte, North Carolina. By 1998 the targeted ministry had grown into a church-within-a-church. And by late 1999 the group was an independent congregation meeting in Charlotte's center-city area.

Pastor Todd Hahn explained that the Warehouse name was inspired by multiple sources, including Acts 2:42, the fact that the warehouse imagery is attractive to busters, and the idea that warehouses are designed to store goods for only a short time before they are distributed once again—a metaphor Hahn thinks is a good one for the church.

Warehouse 242 mixes traditional elements taken from its Evangelical Presbyterian Church denomination with contemporary touches. What's surprising to some young leaders is that the church meets on Sunday mornings, but Hahn said that's what his mostly southern-bred members wanted. Unlike most Presbyterian churches, Warehouse 242 isn't led by committees ("We don't have a single committee in the entire church," he boasted) but by leaders and teams.

Hahn said the church attracts a mix of churched and unchurched people, and he believes that reaching out to folks who have no significant church background is something more churches will need to learn to do in the postmodern era.

"I think we're living in a time of such rapid change and there's such a time of spiritual searching right now," he observed. "It's hard to project out what is going to happen, but what I sense is that the church in North America has lost its home-court advantage. We're now on the margins, or increasingly on the margins, and that is both the most opportune place for us to be and the most dangerous place for us to be.

"The margins are the place where the church has always been the strongest. If the church grabs this moment and is able to be strategic, to depend on God, to think outside the ways it has traditionally thought and to be a missional group of people, then the chance for us to speak back to the culture from the margins is incredibly strong.

"But if we fail, if we are either too conservative or too accommodating, then we will fall right off the margins. It's an incredibly important time for all of us."

Different Churches, Different Approaches

Many churches approach ministry to younger people through regularly scheduled age-specific services, an approach that usually is easier to organize and control than the complicated process of starting a new church within a church or launching a new congregation.

At Calvary Church in Grand Rapids, Michigan, pastor Ed Dobson began an informal Saturday evening service in 1988 where people could feel more relaxed than they did in the more formal Sunday morning services. For Dobson, author of the 1993 book *Starting a Seeker Sensitive Service,* the Saturday evening service was part of an effort to meet people where they were.

By 1996 twenty-something pastor Rob Bell was leading these services, now called Saturday Night, and attended by hundreds of mostly young people. Following his sermons, Bell answered written questions submitted by people in the pews.

"I think what people are yearning for is a place where they don't have to have it all together," Bell told the *New York Times,* calling the Saturday Night service "a safe place to wrestle with the things you really want to wrestle with."[6] A few years later, Calvary Church had spun off Bell's service as a separate church.

And at Willow Creek Community Church, Dieter Zander helped start

Axis, a Saturday evening, Gen X service that began meeting in the church's gymnasium in 1995.

"The boomers, when they came back to church, were looking for answers that would make them better," Zander told *re:generation quarterly* in 1996. "They wanted sermons like 'Five Steps to a Better Marriage.' Generation Xers are more meaning oriented. They want help figuring out what life is about and they don't want sermons on 'five steps to something.' For them, life is way too complicated for that. They don't want easy answers. They want to be given stuff to think about."

In 1996 Zander didn't have a spin-off congregation in mind, saying, "My goal here is to create a safe place for this generation to discover what church will look like for them." By 1999 he had concluded, "The only real hope for the church-within-a-church model is if it is seen as the beginning of a transitional time for a whole church."

And if there is one word that summarizes the period churches are going through at the dawn of the millennium, the word "transitional" probably captures it better than any other.

"We're going to be dancing between the modern and postmodern worlds for maybe the next one hundred years," Ken Baugh observed, "and we'll be experimenting with different models, too.

"We're entering into a new reality, a new worldview. Since the Renaissance, we've never had a major paradigm shift like this," Baugh added. "Right now we're in the blur zone."

new tribes

Forging Networks in a Postdenominational Age

In March 1996 nearly two hundred people involved in ministry to the emerging generations, along with those who were curious about what such ministry might look like, met in Colorado Springs for one of the nation's first broad-based gatherings on the subject. The forum was a bold illustration of the many ways sometimes radical new approaches were bumping against time-tested traditions.

The meeting, called Ministering to Generation X, discussed the direction and shape ministry would take in the twenty-first century, but it was held at a regal, Tudor-style castle that looked like it was built in the eighteenth century. And thanks to the high-decibel praise and worship music led by the band from University Baptist Church in Waco, Texas, the windows of the old building rocked like never before as people stood, swayed, and sang along with the band's musically compelling and lyrically moving song, "There's No Chain."

Organized by Leadership Network, the Dallas-based organization cofounded in 1984 by businessman Bob Buford, the gathering convened at a conference center run by the Navigators, an international parachurch organization founded in 1943 by Dawson Trotman, whose first convert was a U.S. sailor. During the meeting's many open-ended discussion periods, participant after participant expressed dismay about the current state of much of the church in North America. Many young leaders concluded that present-day congregations, Bible colleges, seminaries, and denominations were ill equipped to address the rapidly changing trends in both the world and the church. Nobody suggested burning down all the old institutions, but many seemed to suggest that traditional Christian institutions would be of little value in the future.

"For many of the nearly forty million young people between the ages of eighteen and thirty-four, preachers are like used-car salesmen or politicians," said Ken Baugh, director of the Frontline ministry in McLean, Virginia. "But if your relationships with them are good, and if you are perceived as being authentic, then they'll follow you into the church through the back door."

Pollster George Barna described some of the characteristics of the emerging generation. "This is our first postmodern, post-Christian generation," he said. "They've been immersed in the philosophy of existentialism and the view that there's no objective reality. They're very nonlinear, very comfortable with contradictions, and inclined to view all religions as equally valid."

Chris Seay, a twenty-something, third-generation pastor, had founded University Baptist Church in a movie theater in downtown Waco just a few months before the Colorado conference was held. But his edgy, Sunday-morning services already were attracting nearly 700 people, many of them students at nearby Baylor University who found little of value in the area's traditional congregations.

"This is a generation that has rejected the church, but it hasn't rejected Jesus Christ," said Seay, who wore baggy clothes and sported short-cropped hair and a beard. "The world and this generation are desiring a dialogue with a church that won't listen. This generation is falling through the cracks of Christendom."

Even some of the most recent ecclesiastical innovations were inadequate for meeting the needs of the emerging generations, said Seay. Dieter Zander, who founded New Song Church in Covina, California, before leaving to head up Willow Creek Community Church's buster ministry, spoke for many at the forum when he said, "If you feel like you're fumbling around in the dark, you are."

Decreasing Denominational Loyalties

Independent megachurches like Willow Creek, which operates its own Willow Creek Association of like-minded churches and offers training that competes with seminary offerings, symbolize American evangelicalism's growing move away from denominational loyalties. Emerging young pastors like Seay, who has founded a second Southern Baptist–affiliated congregation—Ecclesia in Houston, Texas—downplay their denominational ties even more than members of the boomer generation did.

This is not to say that denominations are not involved, for they are. Perhaps no one group has started as many Gen X ministries as the Southern Baptist Convention has, but other denominations are helping young leaders launch hundreds of new programs, targeted services, church-within-a-church ministries, and new church plants around the country.*

In cities like Minneapolis, two new congregations founded to reach out to younger people have more in common with each other than they do with their respective denominations.

Spirit Garage (www.spiritgarage.org), launched in 1997 by parent church Bethlehem Lutheran, which is affiliated with the Evangelical Lutheran Church in America, meets in one of the city's urban neighborhoods. "Our commission was to reach young adults in uptown," explained founding pastor Pam Fickenscher, one of the few female pastors in the surprisingly male-dominated world of Gen X ministry.

"Most of our audience either didn't have a strong connection with the faith growing up," Fickenscher said, "or if they had some kind of inkling of church life, they began to have problems with the institutions of the church as soon as they became young adults."

Solomon's Porch (www.solomonsporch.com), which held its first service in January 2000, meets in a renovated loft in Minneapolis's southwest side and is affiliated with the Evangelical Covenant Church. Like Fickenscher, Solomon's Porch pastor Doug Pagitt believes his congregation is reaching people who aren't reached by other churches.

"Many pastors have been trained and equipped to reach two kinds of

---

* A few of the more prominent examples of this trend include Park Street Church in Boston; West Valley Christian Church in West Hills, California; Anchorage Vineyard Christian Fellowship in Alaska; Falls Church Episcopal Church in Virginia; Community Church of Joy in Glendale, Arizona; Fellowship Bible Church in Roswell, Georgia; St. Paul's Lutheran Church in Waukegan, Illinois; Beechwood Reformed Church in Holland, Michigan; Pleasant Hill Seventh-day Adventist Church in Pleasant Hill, California; St. Mark's United Methodist Church in Lincoln, Nebraska; Fellowship Missionary Church in Fort Wayne, Indiana; Maurytown Church of Christ in Erwain, Kentucky; St. Paul's Lutheran Church in Tracy, California; Scottsdale Bible Church in Arizona; Quail Lakes Baptist Church in Stockton, California; Woodmen Valley Chapel in Colorado Springs; and Castle Hills Church Northwest in San Antonio, Texas, where buster pastor Jeff Harris is starting a Gen X ministry in the church where his dad is the senior pastor.

people: either Christian folks who want to grow or nonspiritual people," Pagitt said. "But especially in the younger generation there is an emerging group of people who are very spiritual but are not Christian in orientation. Churches don't know how to deal with these people, who are believers— they just don't believe Christian stuff."

Not only are the post-boomer generations influenced by postmodernism and an increasingly post-Christian culture, they also are postdenominational. Many of them are busy forging new networks and communities that serve many of the purposes denominations used to perform.

Taking the Lead

Bob Buford is the author of the best-selling book *Halftime*, which encourages people to move beyond the selfish concerns of success and survival that can consume their early adult years and focus instead on achieving significance through meaningful service to others.

Buford himself is a model of the life progression he describes. He spent the first half of his life making money in the cable television industry, and he is committed to spending the second half of his life giving much of that money away to help churches and organizations do a better job at ministry.

In 1984, Buford and FedEx executive Fred Smith founded Leadership Network, a nonprofit organization dedicated to encouraging and supporting pastors of large churches through conferences, resources, and other assistance.

Then in the mid-1990s, the same man who was a champion of successful baby boomer megachurches became one of the world's biggest boosters for an embryonic movement of fledgling baby buster pastors. For example, it was Buford's largess that enabled many young pastors to attend the Colorado event described at the beginning of this chapter.

Over the next few years, Leadership Network created a Young Leader Network department (www.youngleader.org) that sponsored other national forums on the future of ministry, as well as a series of smaller regional forums such as 1999's Ministry on the New Edge series, which brought together young leaders for gatherings in Minneapolis; Seattle; Denver; Orange County, California; Washington, D.C.; and Arlington, Texas.

If it sounds surprising that Buford would emerge as a point man for new generations of leaders, he himself is surprised by the way things have turned out. While one might think he pretty much has the emerging generations figured out, Buford admits they leave him baffled and even frustrated. "Sometimes I just can't figure these people out," he has said.

Many older Christian leaders, like Buford, believe it's necessary to turn the keys of the church over to members of the emerging generations, but some of them occasionally worry that the young leaders are going to drive the church off a cliff rather than take it safely down the winding road to the future.

A Forum for the Future

It was a combination of redemptive hope and youthful hubris that led to the founding of the Cambridge, Massachusetts–based Regeneration Forum, one of the most important new groups helping to make connections among emerging Christian leaders.

Cofounder Andy Crouch, now in his early thirties, said that in 1996 there were about half a dozen believers in their twenties who worked for Washington, D.C.–area think tanks like the American Enterprise Institute, the Brookings Institute, the Ethics and Public Policy Center, and the Trinity Forum. These inside-the-beltway believers regularly ran into one another.

Although they came from a variety of Christian traditions, their common interests in faith, culture, and the future of the church and society drew them together, and they founded the Regeneration Forum later that year. The forum's vision is articulated in one of its purpose statements: "We value emerging voices—those who are not being widely heard in the church but who are finding their voice in this generation's appropriation of the Christian tradition."

For Crouch, there was a powerful desire to come together with other young Christians to think about the shape and direction of the church in the twenty-first century.

"We all had a vision for intellectual, cultural, and church renewal, and we believed the new generation had something unique to say to the culture and to the church," he explained. "Of course, when you're young you think you're going to change the world, so you're more inclined to do something stupid like found an organization!"

While most of the major Gen X networking groups are overwhelmingly evangelical in nature, Regeneration Forum is more catholic, attracting leaders from Protestant, Roman Catholic, Orthodox, and Episcopal traditions. In part, that diversity is a reflection of Crouch's own religious pilgrimage.

Raised in a mainstream Episcopal family, he came to a deeper faith in Christ during his high-school years thanks to a youth group that met on Tuesday evenings. Then, as a student at the University of Virginia, where professor James Davison Hunter was an influential mentor, Crouch attended Falls Church Episcopal Church, even though, he noted, "I was more evangelical than Episcopal."

In part that's because he was becoming increasingly convinced of the utter importance of institutions like marriage and the family at a time when his own denomination was becoming more liberal on issues of sexuality and morality. These concerns, along with a growing conviction that tradition was an essential ingredient of ecclesiology—and one that usually was minimized or overlooked in most post-Reformation denominations—led to Crouch's growing fascination with Catholicism. In 1995 he was accepted into the Roman Catholic Church. Today, Regeneration Forum seeks to help connect young believers from various Christian traditions.

The group probably is best known for its acclaimed magazine, *re:generation quarterly* (www.regenerator.com), which strives to provide readers with "thoughtful writing that engages in a sustained conversation rather than speaking superficially to the apparent urgencies of the moment."

The magazine must be doing something right. It not only has been hailed by many Christian leaders as one of the most thoughtful and stimulating of the hundreds of Christian periodicals currently available in the United States, but it also has won kudos from the alternative monthly, *Utne Reader*. In 1999, *re:generation quarterly* was named the winner of *Utne Reader*'s Eleventh Annual Alternative Press Awards in the Spiritual Coverage category, where it beat out the Buddhist magazine *Tricycle,* the pagan publication *PanGaia,* and *Lilith,* a progressive Jewish women's magazine. Crouch couldn't have been happier.

"We were thrilled to have been chosen by *Utne* for this award," he said. "The fact that a 'Christian' magazine could have been listed among these finalists and then chosen for best spiritual coverage means that we are succeeding in our goals of representing and respecting people who are different from ourselves."

Making Connections

Some folks would be pleased with that and stop there, but not the Regeneration Forum, which has its sights set on higher goals. In short, the forum seeks to put its slogan—"community transforming culture"—into action by helping people around the country connect with each other. In order to do that, it sponsors RQ Forums, which consist of fifteen community-based gatherings of people in various parts of the country who read *re:generation quarterly* and want to discuss its ideas. RQ Forum meetings, which usually are held in people's houses, have brought Christians of all stripes together.

"We've seen Republican and Democratic staffers having a civil—even humble—conversation about the Christian Coalition's vision of political engagement," said Bill Haley, who organizes the forums. "We've seen Roman Catholics and Campus Crusade-style evangelicals asking each other the questions they'd always had about the other's tradition. We've seen feminists and traditionalists find fascinating common ground as they talked about the Christian view of the body."

Regeneration Forum also helps make connections on a national scale through its annual Vine events (www.the-vine.org). The Vine, first held over the 1999 Labor Day weekend, brought 250 people to Lake Geneva, Wisconsin, where they participated in a unique gathering. Instead of spending hours listening to "experts" drone on and on, everybody who registered for the event made a brief presentation in one of the weekend's dozens of break-out panel sessions. Notes from these panel sessions can be found at a special Web site (www.the-vine.org/session_notes.html).

"I have been excited by the e-mails I have received about how the connections that were made at The Vine are still growing," said Jennifer Jukanovich, who organized the first event. "We want to help make sure that people can stay connected and can help one another with their respective work. This is how we can show we are one—by the body of Christ working together."

In a promotional e-mail for the 2000 event, Jukanovich promised that it would be just as low-key and lay-centered as the 1999 Vine. "An amazingly diverse group of young leaders will gather to hear from absolutely no name-brand speakers, worship under the leadership of absolutely no best-selling phenom, and attend seminars by absolutely no newly-signed-to-a-multi-book-contract authors. Which is not to say that some of those folks won't be there—they just won't be there with their VIP hats on, but rather as one more participant in the only fully participant-led conference we know of for emerging Christian leaders, animated by Jesus' prayer in John 17 'that they all would be one.'"

Read All About It

re:generation quarterly is far from the only Christian magazine targeting the emerging generations. Nearly half a dozen new print magazines and on-line newsletters have been launched in an effort to inform and serve an audience that feels ignored by mainstream Christian periodicals.

Most of them are struggling to find an audience, which isn't entirely surprising. Media analysts believe that print publications face tough going during an era when young people are bombarded by so many other kinds of mass media. Still, these publications reveal something important about the concerns of the new generations.

Beyond (www.beyondmag.com), published quarterly by a Canadian company, bills itself as "the magazine for people who think about God and want to find out more." Launched in 1995 by an Xer named Karen Neudorf and a few of her friends, the magazine seeks to be a forum for some of the uncertainties of life and faith that aren't always welcomed in church.

"All we knew was we were in the church and we were starving," Neudorf told the *Dallas Morning News.* "We were starving for art, for thought, for something that just wasn't there."[1]

Issue ten of the magazine featured a series of articles on the subject of death, which the cover story called "The Great Unmentionable." Most issues feature essays, poetry, and a catchy graphic layout.

The editors of *FaithWorks* (www.faithworks.com) aren't starving, since they enjoy the support of Associated Baptist Press, an independent publishing company serving Baptists of various denominations. Executive Editor Greg Warner admits to being a boomer, but he says he feels a greater sense of connection with busters.

FaithWorks is an intelligent, attractive magazine that has done some intriguing articles on sexuality, religious themes in movies, the growing popularity of Celtic spirituality, and the validity of sending Christian kids to public schools. Even though the magazine is full of ads for Baptist churches and organizations, it has published articles questioning Baptist orthodoxy.

Echo (www.echomagazine.com) is a quarterly magazine with the goal of "reflecting Jesus to the world." Michael Schwartz, the publication's thirty-one-year-old founding associate editor, grew up Jewish before converting to Christianity. Each issue focuses on a particular theme, such as image consciousness or hate.

Focus on the Family, which in addition to its flagship monthly publishes nearly a dozen targeted magazines for young people, single parents, and Christian activists, launched the *Boundless* E-zine (www.Boundless.org) in 1999. Aimed at college students, the on-line magazine explores a wide range of topics while staying true to its parent organization's conservative values.

And in an age when many young people prefer on-line versions of publications over their "dead tree versions," the Web promises to be the place where many new "publications" and networks will blossom.

Catching Up with a Culture Shift

Established denominations, parachurch organizations, publishers, and even newer ministries are striving to keep up with rapid cultural change. One new Gen X network called the Ooze described some of this change on its Web site (*www.theooze.com*).

> At the dawn of a new millennium, something is oozing just beyond the horizon. The ooze is spreading through-

out the world as new churches are burgeoning into existence. These communities of believers are welling up from
a new movement of God to reach the postmodern world.
We believe that ministry will take on a whole new face as
the Church wakes up to the fact that postmodernism has
seeped into every facet of our society. And that's OK. In
reality, ooze is not easily controlled, harnessed, or re-
strained. Yet, as we begin to embrace the reality of our
times, we have the potential to be a church in transition
from modernism into postmodernism. We see our role as
not trying to define or direct but to be a search party and
tour guides for postmoderns by postmoderns, as we take
the ride of our lives together on this spiritual journey.

Founded by Spencer Burke, a former pastor at Mariner's Church in
Newport Beach, California, and David Trotter, a member of Rock Harbor
Church in Costa Mesa, California (see chapter 10), the Ooze heralded the
arrival of the postmodern church and sponsored its first national gathering
in 1999. In May 2000 the group sponsored the Soularize conference
on worship and the arts, which brought hundreds of people to Southern
California, where they participated in creative worship experiences and
heard talks from people like Leonard Sweet and Sally Morgenthaler
(*www.theooze.com/Pages/OE/OEsoularize.html*).

Jason Mitchell is the director of Leadership Network's Young Leader
Network. His job is to travel throughout the country to meet with young
pastors, encourage and critique them, and help them connect with other
like-minded leaders. Mitchell believes change will be one of the only

constants in North American ministries—at least for a while—as Christians seek fresh ways to sow the seeds of the gospel.

"I think we're going to see some serious adjustments," said Mitchell, a thirty-seven-year-old former church planter. "I think we're going to see some death in some ministries, some slow handing off in others, and some transition. And I don't think all of it is going to be clean.

"But I am optimistic," he continued. "And if you ask me if I'm excited about doing ministry and being engaged in ministry at this time in my life, I've never been more excited because I think there are opportunities. I have the heart of an evangelist, so in some sense, trying to cultivate spirituality in people around the gospel and the message and story of Christ at a time when people are very open to spiritual things is exciting."

bridging the gap

Leaders and Mentors

One reason why Chris Seay never wanted to be a pastor was because he had seen too many pastors' families at close range.

"Seventy-five percent of the pastors' kids I knew had a pretty strong sense of disillusionment," Seay explained. "There was a feeling that their parents were two different sets of people: one at church and one at home. That led to a lot of rebellion and other problems."

Seay grew up in a pastor's family, but his parents were different from the others. "My parents were just who they were, whether they were at church or at home," he said.

Ed Seay was a pastor's kid himself, so he knew the potential pitfalls. He and his wife, Cindy, did everything they could to avoid the problems while raising Chris and their other children.

"From the very beginning, we encouraged the kids to seek out who it was that Christ had made them to be, not what we expected them to be,"

Ed said. "We tried to stress the importance of a solid, godly self-esteem, and we tried to communicate that through unconditional love."

Of course, there were struggles. And Ed insists that Chris was the original inspiration for James Dobson's book *The Strong-Willed Child.*

"We allowed each child to make mistakes and learn from them, within reasonable parameters, instead of trying to pounce on them before they could make a mistake," Ed explained. "We tried to treat them with respect and dignity and not erect artificial boundaries or do things that they would see as inauthentic."

Ed and Cindy consciously practiced consistent discipline, but they didn't force their kids to live up to all the expectations of other church people. They also tried to model transparency in the midst of life's troubles and run the household with common sense and balance.

But if you ask Chris what his dad did right, he has a simple answer. "He gave me permission to color outside the lines," recalled Chris, who is now the pastor of Ecclesia in Houston. "I never felt any pressure from my dad to act like somebody I wasn't. He showed me how to live the Christian life in an authentic way."

On Father's Day 1992, Chris, along with his brothers Brian and Robbie and his sister Jennifer, wrote letters describing "What My Parents Did Right," and gave them to Ed and Cindy. Chris's letter overflowed with gratefulness to his parents.

"You both allowed me to make mistakes and be myself, despite my extreme tendencies. And in time those areas have matured into my strengths."

He thanked his mother for her encouragement. "It is your love and affirmation that created in me the confidence that I can do anything (God willing) that I set my mind to."

And he expressed his appreciation to his father for giving him a healthy model for balancing the often conflicting demands of family and ministry. "Dad, it is by your example of devoted love to Mom that I pray I will care for my wife.... [For you, family] always came first. And now that I understand how demanding ministry can be, I don't know how you did it. I only hope that I can be that same kind of father, whether I serve a church of 20 or 20,000."

The way Ed and Chris related to each other is a beautiful model of how emerging young leaders would like older leaders to treat them: with plenty of love, respect, and freedom.

Profiles of Leadership

It shouldn't come as a major surprise that the shape of Christian leadership is changing in the twenty-first century. Change has been one of the constants in the ways pastors and evangelists have ministered during the first twenty centuries of Christian history.

Jesus and Paul, the two major figures in the church's earliest years, were hands-on practitioners. Jesus chose twelve disciples, and he invested his life in them for three years. He gave much less personal attention to the seventy, whom he commissioned and sent out to do ministry, and even less to the multitudes, who sometimes came to hear him speak or halfheartedly followed him in the hopes that they might get some free fish or bread.

Paul was both an evangelist and a pastor. He could speak to the non-Christian throngs, as he did on Mars Hill, but he also devoted immense amounts of time and energy in shepherding some of the young congregations he had founded and in guiding key leaders like Timothy, to whom

Paul wrote these words: "And the things you have heard me say in the presence of many witnesses entrust to reliable men who will also be qualified to teach others" (2 Timothy 2:2).

Between Paul's time and our own, the church has developed a variety of leadership models that have reflected many of the cultural and historical trends of successive periods. For centuries, as the church adapted to an age of empires, Roman Catholic popes and Eastern Orthodox patriarchs patterned themselves and their large organizations after the style of worldly emperors. Centuries later, America's Great Awakening gave increasing prominence to charismatic evangelists and revivalists, whose powerful impact still can be seen in the homiletical approach of many traditional-style preachers.

In the twentieth century, pastors had to adapt to any number of powerful social forces, such as the growing popularity of psychology and therapy. As more pastors received training in counseling, many adapted a therapeutic model in their relationships with members as well as in their preaching. Psychology also changed the way many pastors preached. Whereas revivalist preachers branded moral failings as sin, pastors influenced by psychology typically described such failings as a result of various kinds of brokenness.

From Good Shepherd to Ecclesiastical CEO

Perhaps the most important change to affect pastors in recent decades was the rise of a type of leader who might best be described as the "ecclesiastical CEO." Unlike the pastoral, agrarian images that come to mind when one hears Jesus describing himself as the Good Shepherd, the ecclesiastical

CEO's techniques, style, and bottom-line, consumer-oriented approach are heavily influenced by the models of leadership most highly acclaimed in the corporate world.

Virtually all of the pastors who have been hailed as most "successful" (which, by the way, is a term the New Testament never applies to pastors or other church leaders) have won such kudos by becoming rulers of their respective religious domains. Success is typically measured by attendance or membership figures, numbers of staff and programs, the size of church budgets or physical plants, and the number of books, videos, radio programs, and speaking engagements the CEO pastor has produced.

Has this shift from a pastoral model to the ecclesiastical CEO model been good for the church? Undoubtedly, better management techniques have helped some churches become more effective in serving God and their communities. But the shift in approaches also has left a legacy of success-driven pastors who frequently burn out and megachurches that are more broad than they are deep. One thing's for sure: Many emerging leaders are seeking different models as they begin pastoring their flocks.

Emerging Leadership Styles

So far there's no crystal-clear picture of what leadership will look like in the current millennium, but it's clear that a shift is under way.

Brad Sargent of Golden Gate Theological Seminary recently wrote an article in which he discussed "the essence of postmodern leadership." In the article, he examined the contrasting approaches of "modern" and "postmodern" leaders.

"Modern leaders think categorically and sequentially," Sargent wrote.

They seem to like everything divided down to nice, neat compartments, and they exceed at crafting three-point sermon outlines with alliterative key words and occasional acronyms. They've taken the best of social science research methods and corporate leadership styles and applied them to the task of church growth. They've also given the Church denominations and parachurch agencies, mission programs, and all kinds of study tools for spiritual growth....

Postmodern leaders think in webs of relationships and multiple layers of meaning. As leaders, they offer the Church a gift of rejuvenation in a confusing culture that has more in common with the pagan first century than the later Enlightenment era. They can stand on the verge of chaos and complexity, and find it energizing instead of frightening. They can sit with hurting people in all their emotional pain and not feel compelled to get them into a self-help healing program. They realize that people's wounds are relational in nature, and that informational solutions alone will never be enough to remove this brokenness. They can live within the paradoxical tension of wanting to impact the world, yet often see that their lives are lived in small arenas. But they persevere because God has called them to be His faithful servants, not 'successful' servants.[1]

In *Generating Hope,* Jimmy Long made similar distinctions between typical postmodern and modern (or Enlightenment) leadership styles:

ENLIGHTENMENT	POSTMODERN
positional	earned
perfect	wounded healer
supervisory	mentoring
product-oriented	process-oriented
individual	team
dictatorial	participatory
aspiring	inspiring
controlling	empowering[2]

One thing is becoming increasingly clear: Emerging leaders are boldly applying their unique core values to the issues of leadership, and what they're coming up with promises to remake the church.

From CEO to Soul Mate

One of the most powerful images of the older generation of leaders is the pastor standing alone on a megachurch stage and orating to a large and largely passive audience. In such circumstances the emphasis is on public performance, and few members of the church get to peek behind the curtain to see what their pastor is really made of.

But many members of the emerging generations are skeptical about such leaders. Like the respondents to a 1999 Gallup poll that asked, "Which professions are the most honest?" they give the clergy less than stellar marks. In the poll, 56 percent of respondents said that the clergy were generally honest. That means they ranked behind nurses, pharmacists, veterinarians, medical doctors, and K-12 teachers.

Members of Generation X value authenticity, a characteristic that is as difficult to define as it is to live out. But there's no doubting that it's a value that hasn't been given top priority in the lives of many ecclesiastical CEOs. Authentic leaders place a greater emphasis on transparency and honesty— both with themselves and others—than on either public performance or political agility. And they also strive to place a greater priority on understanding and living out the gospel than they do on packaging it and proclaiming it to others.

Sally Morgenthaler believes future leaders will place a greater emphasis on the hidden dimensions of the interior life than on the glittering image of public performance.

"One of the most important things you can do if you're working with postmoderns is to develop an interior life and to face your dragons," she suggested. "And that is very difficult when you work in a church because we are actually taught not to face our dragons. Image has become so important, especially if you're a leader, that you really can't have 'stuff' going on in your life.

"Now, you can talk about the fact that you have 'stuff' if you're preaching," she added. "It's really cool to touch on it two-thirds of the way through your sermon in an opportune moment if it might affect people. We tend to be okay with manipulating people that way. But most of the time, we like to hide—and hide from ourselves first and foremost."

Preacher Performers to Wounded Healers

Morgenthaler and others note that many leaders have bought into and promote a model of leadership that portrays pastors as theologically astute, psychologically integrated, spiritually mature, emotionally self-contained, morally superior, and physically attractive. But such a model comes at a high price.

"There are a lot of things we lose when we do that," Morgenthaler warned. "We lose our authenticity, we lose our ability to speak to people, and we lose the value of our journey, our pain, and our confusion. Sometimes I wish we as leaders could say we don't have a clue about this subject or that subject. I think that if we could use three little words, 'I don't know,' this would speak volumes."

Often people seem to want their leaders to be flawless and all-knowing. Morgenthaler described her experience in speaking to a church group recently. As she spoke, she shared some of the difficulties she had been going through at the time. But unlike many Christian stories of sorrow and woe, she didn't "put a bow on it at the end." Some of her listeners were shocked at her honesty and disappointed with her realism.

"Most of us have accepted that it is not okay to not be okay in the Christian community," she observed. "But where does that leave the gut-level honesty David exhibited in the Psalms? David repeatedly cries out, 'God why did you do this? I don't understand this. I feel terrible about this.' In fact, there are more laments in the Psalms than there are praises and celebrations.

"In much of the modern church world, we have left out lament. When I look at some of the praise choruses that have been written, I have a hard time finding stuff for Good Friday. There's nothing about the crucifixion, and everything's about Easter."

While this kind of ever-upbeat approach has been successful with some people, Morgenthaler and others who work with members of the emerging generations say its days are numbered.

"They've lived tragedies, and if all you say to them is that the world is a nice place, they're going to scream at you any way they can, through their music, with graffiti, or by piercing their bodies."

Public Roles, Private Lives

One pastor of a Gen X church went through a painful ecclesiastical ordeal in 1999. He had to ask his worship leader to step down after months of personality conflicts and tense Sunday mornings. But instead of quietly dismissing the man and sweeping the issue under the rug, the pastor and the entire church walked through the experience with the leader and allowed it to be a learning experience for the entire community.

"The worship leader who had been leading our band for the last two years needed to step down, and I had to be the one to initiate it," said the pastor. "It was the hardest thing I've done since our church started, but it was necessary. I didn't exactly go about it in the best way, and we have worked through that, but the change has been good. On a recent Sunday he got up and apologized for not being more honest about his spiritual state and hiding behind the role of worship leader. It was a huge thing to do. I'm proud of him. It was something the whole church needed to experience.

"I then spoke about confession, accountability, forgiveness, and honesty. Then we had one of our usual reflective communion services. With the lights out and the candles on, people came up and knelt on the carpet in prayer before they took communion. It was great. It seems like God is using this situation for some healing in our church.

"I've learned some powerful lessons in the midst of this whole deal," the pastor concluded. "I could've handled the situation better and have learned not to take the spiritual state of my leaders for granted. I am reminded that God wants to shape my character as much as everyone else's in this crazy church. I am humbled at my inadequacies. As I've said many times, I am often amazed that this church still exists in spite of me. I'm liking more and more getting out of the way and letting God move."

Pastors as Philosophers

Just as earlier social transformations forced pastors to be counselors, today's wrenching cultural changes are encouraging many younger pastors to be philosophers.

"You cannot interpret the signs of the times," said Jesus, who was in the habit of upbraiding the "blind" Pharisees (Matthew 16:3). Today's young leaders are committed to reading and interpreting their culture as previous generations were to reading and interpreting their Bibles and commentaries. While the older CEO model of pastoral leadership values efficiency over metaphysical might, many emerging leaders believe philosophical insight can help them pastor during turbulent times.

Brad Cecil, the pastor of "aXXes" in San Antonio, Texas, described his own mid-1990s journey toward more introspection and speculation.

"I was traveling down the ministry road that I had traveled on for years," he began,

> but one day I ran into a sign that read "Detour." Like so many others in ministry, I had witnessed the exodus of adults from our church, and apart from programs that had ancillary attraction (such as meeting other single people), I didn't see much activity among the young adults.
>
> However, I saw this growing spirituality in popular culture, *especially* among young adults, and was confused. I began to sense that young adults were not just "going through a phase" that they would grow out of some day before "finding their way back to the church."
>
> It seemed that something had happened to the way people think. The signs on this detour kept pointing me in a direction off the main road. My detour became an intense theological-philosophical journey.
>
> I started exploring the issue of postmodernity and its effect on our culture. I started to uncover "understanding" that helped explain this emerging spirituality, pluralism, desire for dialogue, and real community that was so prevalent in young adults. But to be honest, I heard little or no discussion of it in ministry circles and felt fairly alone on this detour.[3]

Soon Cecil was discussing the things he was learning with other pastors, but the discussion didn't stop there. He also talked with members of his church about postmodernism, what it was, and what its implications might be for their lives.

Earlier generations of Christian leaders didn't always do too well with helping laypeople understand and respond to cultural and philosophical trends, often settling for setting up straw men, like "secular humanism," and persuading everyone that it was bad and they should stay away from it.

Now that postmodernism has thoroughly worked its way into the fabric of American culture, young pastors like Cecil have decided to spend more of their energy understanding the times and helping their members do likewise, thus empowering them to go out into the world, aware but unafraid.

Finding Their Way

One doesn't know whether to laugh or cry at Douglas Coupland's portrayal of a buster's complaint about his confining workplace cubicle (also called a "veal-fattening pen") and his horrible job: "I work from eight till five in front of a sperm-dissolving VDT performing abstract tasks that indirectly enslave the Third World."

But this depiction does speak volumes for many young people, whether they're dealing with the bureaucracies of the workplace or the church. Bruce Tulgan, the Gen X author of *Managing Generation X*, describes his cohorts' feelings about their position in the work world: "No matter how talented any one of us might be, most Xers feel like disposable labor—the paper plates of the job market."

Many older workers have concluded that members of Gen X are merely self-centered slackers, but in his "Memo to managers of Generation X,"

Tulgan begins by telling them to "abandon the slacker myth." He also explains many Xers' seemingly contradictory feelings about work.

"What Xers are not willing to do is to pay dues which, in any sense, are based on protocols of hierarchy or rights of initiation," Tulgan wrote. "The reason is clear—the traditional rites in the workplace have been part of an initiation to a club called job security, a club which Xers are not invited to join. For that reason, Xers are not willing to embrace the bottom rung of the ladder as a matter of course, despite the fact that those of predecessor generations may have done so."

Rather than slaving for their task-oriented masters, Xers would prefer to learn from caring mentors.

Seeking Mentors

Marcus Robinson is the youth pastor at Parker Christian Center, an Assemblies of God congregation in Colorado. Over the last few years, he has become increasingly convinced that young people want and need mentors, and in 1999 he preached a sermon in which he pleaded with older believers to reach out to the congregation's younger members.

He began with his own amplified version of a passage from John's first epistle: "I write to you, dear children [all of us in the church], because your sins have been forgiven on account of his name. I write to you, fathers [all of the seasoned, mature believers], because you have known him who is from the beginning. I write to you, young men [all you new believers], because you have overcome the evil one. I write to you, dear children [all of us in the church], because you have known the Father. I write to you, fathers, because you have known him who is from the beginning. I write to you, young men, because you are strong, and the word of God lives in you, and you have overcome the evil one" (1 John 2:12-14).

He then argued that both older and younger members of Christ's body need each other.

"Experience can lead to strength, but it can also lead to rigidity and stagnation, and little action. Youthful enthusiasm can lead to busyness and change, but it can also lead to little effective action. John wanted us to see that we needed each other. The battle we are engaged in will require zeal and youthful strength but also wisdom and maturity. If we are to fight successfully, we need both."

Todd Hahn and David Verhaagen agree, as they wrote in their book *GenXers After God:* "We believe that Gen Xers are most in need of comrades, friends who can move intimately through life with them." And calling on elders to take up the task, they wrote, "Model and teach what it means to be loyal in friendship and why it is important to speak the truth in love."[4]

Letting Them Lead

In addition to older comrades, members of the emerging generations need opportunities to serve their own. Jason Mitchell of Leadership Network has seen more than his share of potential young leaders who haven't been given the chance to fulfill their calling. He encourages church leaders to give them a chance.

"If I could say one thing to a group of senior pastors who have control over buildings and budgets, I would say that when your young person comes to you and says, 'I want to start an alternative service or a church-within-a-church,' that they would hear him like they would hear a Korean pastor who wants to use the building at two o'clock on Sunday afternoons.

"I would challenge them to completely release control of that thing and embrace whatever vision comes out of it, because when a Korean guy wants to use the building to reach his own group, it's kind of like, 'Hey, we've got this cool Korean church and they have communion every Sunday, and they eat dinner every time they have church, and that's different from what we do but we don't care, because that's a particular culture that we can't reach as well as they can.'

"I hope they are just as open to the guy who comes and wants to start the alternative church. But often established leaders are reluctant to release that control."

Caught between the past and the future, many young leaders want to reinvent the church for their own generations. And if they don't do it in existing buildings, they will do it somewhere else. Either way, these emerging leaders are the architects of the church of the future, and Mitchell and others say it's time to let them start designing it.

It's too early to tell what this future church will look like, but it's unlikely that the emerging generations will either radically reinvent Christianity—as some of their optimistic boosters believe—or drive it into extinction——as some of their harshest critics fear. Instead, it's more likely that they will modify Christianity with their unique generational and cultural perspectives, much like believers have been doing throughout the first two thousand years of church history.

acknowledgments

There are many people who graciously helped me as I was working on this project. My wife, Lois, as always, helped me at every step of the way.

Bob Buford, Brad Smith, and Carol Childress of Leadership Network helped introduce many of the leaders and groups covered in this book to each other and to me. That includes Chris Seay, whom I met at a 1995 Leadership Network conference and who has been a friend and encourager ever since.

Literary agent Greg Johnson shared my passion for this project and persuaded Dan Rich of WaterBrook Press to publish it. Others at WaterBrook, including Laura Barker, Ron Lee, and Thomas Womack, helped guide and shape this project.

Jerry Jones gave me videotapes of the detailed interviews he conducted with Ken Baugh, Mark Driscoll, and Sally Morgenthaler as part of a documentary project he was doing for Cook Communications Ministries. And Brandon Unger helped with tons of research.

Some of the material in this book originally appeared, in slightly different form, in articles published in the following sources: *Christianity Today,* Religion News Service, *Leadership,* the *Dallas Morning News, Charisma, Pastor's Family, Youthworker Journal,* and *Worship Leader.* The author would like to thank the editors.

notes

Chapter One

1. Pat Robertson, *The Turning Tide* (Dallas: Word, 1993), 203-4.

2. David Ashley Morrison, "Beyond the Gen X Label," *Brandweek,* 17 March 1997.

3. Douglas Rushkoff, *The GenX Reader* (New York: Ballantine, 1994), 4.

4. William Strauss and Neil Howe, "The New Generation Gap," *Atlantic Monthly,* December 1992, as published in Rushkoff, *The GenX Reader,* 293.

5. J. Walker Smith as quoted by Margot Hornblower in "Great Expectations," *Time,* 9 June 1997.

6. Richard Miniter, "Generation X Does Business," *American Enterprise,* July-August 1997.

7. Jeff Bantz, "Generation X, Implications for Mission Organizations of the Sociological Distinctives of Christians Born Between 1961 and 1975," *Next,* April 1996.

8. Dieter Zander, "The Gospel for Generation X: Making Room in the Church for 'Busters,'" *Leadership,* Spring 1995.

9. Andres Tapia, "Reaching the First Post-Christian Generation," *Christianity Today,* 12 September 1994, 23.

10. Andy Crouch, "Generation Complex," *re:generation quarterly* 5, no. 3 (1999): 3.

Chapter Two

1. Peter F. Drucker, *Post-Capitalist Society* (New York: HarperBusiness, 1993), 1.

2. Vann Wesson, *Generation X Field Guide and Lexicon* (San Diego: Orion Media, 1997), 132.

3. Douglas Rushkoff, *The GenX Reader* (New York: Ballantine, 1994), 7.

4. Jefferson Morley, "Twentysomething," in Rushkoff, *The GenX Reader.*

5. Stanley Grenz, *A Primer on Postmodernism* (Grand Rapids, Mich.: Eerdmans, 1996), 4.

6. Grenz, *A Primer on Postmodernism,* 41.

7. Grenz, *A Primer on Postmodernism,* 43.

8. Tom Wolf, "The Urban Church and the Post-Modern World," *NetFax,* 5 January 1997.

9. Robert Bellah, Richard Madsen, William M. Sullivan, Ann Swidler, and Steven M. Tipton, *Habits of the Heart* (New York: Harper and Row, 1985), 221.

10. Harvey Cox, "Jesus and Generation X," presented at "Jesus at 2000," Twenty-seventh National Conference of Trinity Institute 1996, New York (New York: Office of Video Production, Parish of Trinity Church).

11. Wade Clark Roof, *Spiritual Marketplace: Baby Boomers and the Remaking of American Religion* (Princeton, N.J.: Princeton University Press, 1999), 128.

12. Roof, *Spiritual Marketplace,* 23.

13. Roof, *Spiritual Marketplace,* 9.

14. Roof, *Spiritual Marketplace,* 48.

15. Roof, *Spiritual Marketplace,* 130.

Chapter Four

1. Robert Banks, "Individual," in *The Complete Book of Everyday Christianity*, edited by Banks and R. Paul Stevens (Downers Grove, Ill.: InterVarsity, 1997), 524.

2. Jimmy Long, *Generating Hope* (Downers Grove, Ill.: InterVarsity, 1997), 50.

3. Long, *Generating Hope*, 61.

4. Long, *Generating Hope*, 84.

5. William Mahedy and Janet Bernardi, *A Generation Alone* (Downers Grove, Ill.: InterVarsity, 1994), 72.

6. Mahedy and Bernardi, *A Generation Alone*, 78.

7. Mahedy and Bernardi, *A Generation Alone*, 80.

8. As quoted in Laura Sessions Stepp, "Parents Are Alarmed by an Unsettling New Fad in Middle Schools: Oral Sex," *Washington Post*, 8 July 1999.

Chapter Five

1. Henry Blackaby as quoted in "New Movements of God in the U.S.," *Leadership Network Explorer*, 28 February 2000.

2. Robert Webber, *Ancient-Future Faith* (Grand Rapids, Mich.: Baker, 1999).

Chapter Six

1. Calvin Miller as quoted in "Preaching in Today's Culture," *NetFax*, 15 February 1999.

2. Bob Losyk, "Generation X: What They Think and What They Plan to Do," *The Futurist*, March-April 1997.

3. Todd Hahn and David Verhaagen, *Reckless Hope* (Grand Rapids, Mich.: Baker, 1996), 104.

4. Sundee Frazier as quoted in "Preach Interactively," *Current Thoughts and Trends,* February 1999, 15.

5. George Barna, *Evangelism That Works* (Ventura, Calif.: Regal, 1995), 113-15.

6. Lesslie Newbigin as quoted in George R. Hunsberger and Craig van Gelder, *The Church Between Gospel and Culture. The Emerging Mission in North America* (Grand Rapids, Mich.: Eerdmans, 1996), 302.

7. Donald C. Posterski, *Reinventing Evangelism* (Downers Grove, Ill.: Inter-Varsity, 1994), 15.

8. Posterski, *Reinventing Evangelism,* 122.

Chapter Seven

1. Dante Chinni, "History 101 for Gen Xers," *The Washington Monthly,* June 1997.

2. Trinity Hartman, "Young Activists Take Detour Past Politics," Knight Ridder News Service, 19 March 1999.

3. William Mahedy and Janet Bernardi, *A Generation Alone* (Downers Grove, Ill.: InterVarsity, 1994), 97.

4. Holly J. Lebowitz, "A Resurrection of Campus Activism," *Sojourners Online,* September-October 1999.

5. David L. Marcus, "Generation X Turns Out to Be Generous," *U.S. News and World Report,* 21 February 2000.

Chapter Eight

1. Kevin Smith as quoted in David Kehr, "Deflator of Faith? Director Begs to Differ," *New York Times,* 1 August 1999.

2. Kevin Smith as quoted on the *ZUG* Web site (www.zug.com), 5 April 1999.

3. Todd Hahn and David Verhaagen, *GenXers After God* (Grand Rapids, Mich.: Baker, 1998), 62-3.

4. Jason Baker, *Christian Cyberspace Companion* (Grand Rapids, Mich.: Baker, 1995), 17.

5. Walt Wilson as quoted in "The Internet Church," *Explorer,* 17 January 2000.

6. John Carley as quoted in "The '640 x 480' Window" on the Web site www.theooze.com.

7. Jeff Zaleski, *The Soul of Cyberspace* (New York: HarperSanFrancisco, 1997), 9.

8. Erik Davis, "The God Squad," *Spin,* January 1999.

9. Jon Pareles, "Building an Album Out of Scraps and Feelings," *New York Times,* 18 September 1999.

10. Scott Stapp as quoted in "Creed Interview," *Next,* February 1999 special edition, 9.

11. Bill Moyers and George Lucas, "Of Myth and Men," *Time*.com, 26 April 1999, 2.

12. Kendall Hamilton and Devin Gordon, "Waiting for Star Wars," *Newsweek*.com, 1 February 1999.

Chapter Nine

1. Joseph Bayly, *The Gospel Blimp* (Grand Rapids, Mich.: Zondervan, 1960), 78.

2. George Barna, *Marketing the Church* (Colorado Springs: NavPress, 1988), 23.

3. Barna, *Marketing the Church,* 37.

4. Barna, *Marketing the Church,* 26-33.

5. Keith Page as quoted in Elaine Gale, "(Punk) Rock of Ages," *Los Angeles Times*, 17 July 2000.

6. Rob Bell as quoted in Gustav Niebuhr, "A Question About God? Just Hand It to the Usher," *New York Times*, 1 September 1996.

Chapter Ten

1. Karen Neudorf as quoted in Kevin Eckstrom, "Gen-X Voices: New Magazine Faces One Generation's Issues," *Dallas Morning News*, 22 May 1999.

Chapter Eleven

1. Brad Sargent, "The Essence of Postmodern Leadership: Four Kinds of Kingdom Workers in the Postmodern Era," unpublished article.

2. Jimmy Long, *Generating Hope* (Downers Grove, Ill.: InterVarsity, 1997), 152-53.

3. Brad Cecil, "Detour," *Next*, February 1999, 2.

4. Todd Hahn and David Verhaagen, *GenXers After God* (Grand Rapids, Mich.: Baker, 1998), 147.